Grand Canyon

AMERICA'S NATIONAL PARKS

AMERICA'S NATIONAL PARKS SERIES

Char Miller, Pomona College
Series Editor

America's National Parks promotes the close investigation of the complex and often contentious history of the nation's many national parks, sites, and monuments. Their creation and management raises a number of critical questions from such fields as archaeology, geology and history, biology, political science, and sociology, as well as geography, literature, and aesthetics. Books in this series aim to spark public conversation about these landscapes' enduring value, by probing such diverse topics as ecological restoration, environmental justice, tourism and recreation, tribal relations, the production and consumption of nature, and the implications of wildland fire and wilderness protection. Even as these engaging texts cross interdisciplinary boundaries, they will also dig deeply into the local meanings embedded in individual parks, monuments, or landmarks and locate these special places within the larger context of American environmental culture.

Grand Canyon: A History of a Natural Wonder and National Park
by Don Lago

Grand Canyon

A History of a Natural Wonder and National Park

Don Lago

University of Nevada Press *Reno & Las Vegas*

University of Nevada Press, Reno, Nevada 89557 USA
www. unpress.nevada.edu
Copyright © 2015 by University of Nevada Press
All rights reserved
Manufactured in the United States of America
Design by Kathleen Szawiola

Library of Congress Cataloging-in-Publication Data

Lago, Don, 1956-
Grand Canyon : a history of a natural wonder
and national park / Don Lago.
pages cm. — (America's national parks)
Includes bibliographical references and index.
ISBN 978-0-87417-990-3 (pbk. : alk. paper) —
ISBN 978-0-87417-991-0 (e-book)
1. Grand Canyon (Ariz.)—History. 2. Grand Canyon National Park
(Ariz.)—History. I. Title.
F788.L337 2015
979.1'32—dc23
2015014444

The paper used in this book meets the requirements of American
National Standard for Information Sciences—Permanence of Paper
for Printed Library Materials, ANSI/NISO Z39.48-1992 (R2002). Binding
materials were selected for strength and durability.

This book has been reproduced as a digital reprint.

All photographs courtesy of the Grand Canyon National Park
Museum Collection, unless otherwise noted.

Contents

Illustrations

Preface

The Grand Canyon is all about history. It offers the world's greatest display of geological history, eons of time and events stacked up in an orderly record. Several famous writers, including John Muir and John Wesley Powell, have compared the Grand Canyon's rock strata to the pages of a great book.

The Grand Canyon has inspired humans to write hundreds of books about it, including history books. But surprisingly, there have been very few books that offer a general summary of the canyon's rich human history. This is not because the canyon lacks this history. On the contrary, just as the canyon is larger-than-life, it has attracted many larger-than-life characters and inspired them to many bold, unlikely deeds.

Yet most Grand Canyon history books have been about specialized aspects of it. River running, in particular, is a dramatic, world-class story that continues to inspire new books. Other canyon history books have focused on topics such as Native Americans, American pioneers, the Santa Fe Railway, art, or a few charismatic individuals like John Wesley Powell. Readers looking for a comprehensive yet concise book on Grand Canyon history that covers everything from its geology to the array of interesting characters it has attracted could not find anything at all. This book fills that void. It is for both canyon visitors and history lovers who would like to know the whole story, something about everything. This book was written to be both intellectually sophisticated and enjoyable storytelling. It will be helpful to visitors who have only a day or two at the park and want to have a richer experience of the canyon. The canyon becomes deeper when you know the stories it holds.

Historians have tended to define history as national history, the story of American exploration, pioneering, and settlement. "Real" history was mainly about politics and economics. Grand Canyon history books have tended to follow this tradition. They have treated Native Americans as a mere prelude to "real" history, and they largely left out the stories of scientists, artists, architects, writers, poets, hikers, and river runners encountering the canyon. Yet while the canyon's pioneer days contain some lively people and stories, it was the scientists, cultural leaders, adventurers, and conservationists whose visions of the Grand Canyon have defined the way we experience it today. This book offers a broader view of history, in which the prospector's shovel graduates into the artist's brush and the rafter's oars. The physical exploration of the canyon was only the beginning of the cultural exploration of it.

The Grand Canyon is an enormously complex place, and no one can be an expert on all aspects of it. Yet the canyon has inspired some brilliant people to devote years or careers to it, and this book has benefited from their knowledge and enthusiasm.

Kim Besom, Mike Quinn, and Colleen Hyde of the Grand Canyon National Park Museum Collection are a great asset to the park and to researchers; Mike was especially helpful in finding some of the photographs for this book. Karen Greig did invaluable research in the Bancroft Library. Richard Quartaroli, formerly of Cline Library Special Collections at Northern Arizona University, reviewed this manuscript and made good suggestions and plucked out some errors, but of course any remaining errors are entirely my own.

I appreciated the time, interest, and contributions of Earle Spamer, Mike Anderson, Mary Williams, Roger Clark, Larry Stevens, Linda Jalbert, Jim Babbitt, Terra Waters, Wayne and Helen Ranney, Tom Martin, Hazel Clark, Alan Petersen, Jerry Snow, Bruce Aiken, Jan Balsom, Ellen Brennan, Amy Horn, Brad Dimock, Drifter Smith, Kim Crumbo, Roy Webb, Greg Woodall, Lynn Hamilton, Dave Wegner, Tom Bean, Susan Lamb, Dan and Diane Cassidy, Keith and Nancy Green, Richard and Sherry Mangum, Erik Berg, Lee Lansing, Sharon Hester, Jacqita Bailey, Marker Marshall, Vince Welch, Al Richmond, Antoinette Beiser, Kevin Schindler, Alfredo Conde, Sheri Curtis, Stewart Aitchison, Bruce Shaw, Ron and Pat Brown, Tom Myers, Julie Russell, Stew Fritts, Stephen and Lois Hirst, Matt Goodwin, Michael Ghiglieri, Mary Lois Brown, Virginia Martin, Al Richmond, Henry Karpinski, Marie Jackson, Steve Verkamp, Mike Verkamp, Susan Verkamp, Shane Murphy, and Betty Upchurch.

This book was the idea of Matt Becker at the University of Nevada Press, and I thank him and the rest of the press for guiding the idea into solid form and Annette Wenda for her able editing.

Grand Canyon

Introduction
Reverence and Conquest

Better than anywhere else on Earth, the Grand Canyon offers a deep look—literally—into the forces of creation, into time, geological events, and biological evolution. Nowhere else is Earth's history so well preserved and presented. Other national parks and natural wonders offer only a page or two of this story. They offer one volcanic mountain, or some petrified logs, or a granite valley carved by glaciers in a few seconds by the Grand Canyon's timescale. Instead of a few pages of Earth's story, the Grand Canyon throws the book at you.

The Grand Canyon is also a larger-than-life place for the life that lives there, including humans. The canyon is enormous with challenges. Most animals and plants could not live there. The canyon requires bighorn sheep that can leap up cliffs, condors that can go for two weeks without a meal, and plants that can withstand 120-degree heat and go for months without rain. The canyon also requires extraordinary people; it is a difficult place for humans to explore or to live. Even the Native Americans who lived there found it a demanding home. Most American prospectors took one look into the canyon, saw the trouble it would demand, and turned around and left for easier places. Most artists and poets quickly recognized the futility of trying to portray the canyon. Every year hikers accustomed to easier landscapes—even the Rockies or Alps—suffer terribly in the canyon, and some die. River runners with decades of experience feel a beginner's fear when facing the thunder of Lava Falls.

Yet the Grand Canyon always found a few people who were large enough to match it. If they were ordinary people when they came to the canyon, the canyon had the power to make them extraordinary. The canyon has filled people with extraordinary dreams, emotions, ideas, and efforts. It is a magnificent theater stage that might have been wasted on small characters and small stories.

The canyon has the power to give life. For the Native Americans who

1

lived and farmed inside the Grand Canyon a thousand years ago, the canyon was not just the soil that became their flesh, but their place of creation, where humans first emerged into this world. Their descendants, the Hopis and Zunis, still hold the canyon sacred and make pilgrimages to it. For geologists too, the canyon is a place of creation, revealing the forces that shaped the earth, life, and humans. One of the first geologists to see the canyon, Clarence Dutton, felt it was so powerful that only the names of gods could do justice to its landscapes. For many famous artists, poets, and nature writers, the canyon testified about ultimate realities, about beauty, nature, and God.

Humans have always needed stories to define their identities, including personal, family, group, and national stories, and the most important stories are creation stories, which give humans a sense of their place in the cosmos. The Grand Canyon's first explorer by boat, John Wesley Powell, risked his life to explore its geological creation story. Most tourists today come to the canyon expecting mainly a visual spectacle, but many sense something deeper—both philosophically and spiritually. They get at least a glimpse of the primordial, a creation story written in stone. They define this creation story in different ways, some seeing nature, some seeing God, and some leaving with an expanded sense of nature or God. No other landscape connects so powerfully with the human need for a creation story.

Yet the first story through which most Americans saw the Grand Canyon was not a creation story, but a national story. John Wesley Powell was quite an anomaly among American explorers of the West in being motivated by science; most explorers were acting in the service of national expansion.

Nations need stories to define themselves, and Americans, who lacked the long histories of European nations, felt a more urgent need to define their identity, values, and goals. The guiding American story became that of national expansion, of the "manifest destiny" of a free, brave people to conquer a continent and build a great nation. American heroes were those who served national expansion, such as Daniel Boone and Davy Crockett. Anything that stood in the way of national expansion was defined as bad—the British Empire, Indians, Mexicans, forests, herds of buffalo, deserts, and canyons. By the time Americans and their national story arrived at the Grand Canyon, this story had been validated by a century of tremendous success. The American national story would become one of the most successful and powerful national stories in human history, one that would propel Americans to the moon, fascinate the world with western movies, and mold the values that would guide American society long after the frontier was gone. It would also define the Grand Canyon as a resource to be conquered for the sake of individual and national wealth. Into this theater of primordial forces arrived prospectors, cowboys, loggers, hunters, soldiers, and the builders of railroads, dams, and towns.

Yet the Grand Canyon would not fit willingly into the American national story. The canyon was telling its own powerful story, its creation story. At the canyon the national story and the creation story collided, like tectonic plates, and created a lot of cultural heat, deformation, and ultimately uplift. Much of the cultural and political history of the Grand Canyon was defined by this collision of stories, by Americans struggling to see the canyon as something much more than a frontier to be conquered. Even when Americans decided that creation was more important than consumption, they struggled to figure out a natural wonder that was quite different from anything they or their European ancestors had encountered before.

Americans did have a good intellectual foundation for appreciating nature. America's founding ideals were derived from the Enlightenment and romanticism, both grounded in nature, if in different ways. The Enlightenment said that nature held a rational, clockwork order and that humans were rational beings who were trustworthy to organize human society in a rational way—meaning democratically; it was this tradition that inspired Thomas Jefferson. Romanticism saw nature as a manifestation of divinity, a stone and living testament of the benevolence of creation; it was this tradition that inspired Henry David Thoreau and John Muir. A century after the American Revolution, these two intellectual traditions blended together and generated the idea of national parks, of democratic enclaves where Americans could experience nature's power. But the idea of national parks faced a long uphill struggle, especially for the Grand Canyon, which would not become a national park until nearly a half century after Yellowstone became the first. America's intellectual reverence for nature was no match for the onrushing tide of America's conquest of nature.

Americans had landed on a vast continent that offered abundant farmland, forests, wildlife, and minerals to those bold enough to take them. The frontier seemed limitless, and this bred a culture of greed and waste. Americans clear-cut their forests, poured their irreplaceable topsoil into rivers, and turned magnificent herds of bison into piles of rotting corpses. Americans imagined Yosemite Valley full of grazing sheep, the Grand Canyon full of mines. Both the poor immigrant fresh off the ship and the mining baron in the mansion on the hill saw American nature as merely the raw material for obtaining wealth.

The two American visions of nature, nature as inspiration and nature for conquest, often coexisted and contended within the same individuals. Thomas Jefferson loved natural history and directed Lewis and Clark to document it on their expedition, but he sent them west mainly to spearhead national expansion. Walt Whitman celebrated America's great trees, but he also loved the sounds of axes and saws and hammers. Teddy Roosevelt campaigned to protect the Grand Canyon, but as a hunter he helped push its mountain lions toward extinction. The same Gilded Age railroad companies that exploited and enraged millions of people also fought to establish and defend national parks, and they became the generous patrons of visionary artists and architects.

These contending visions of nature, reverence and conquest, would meet and clash energetically at the Grand Canyon and generate both inspiration and indignation. Yet neither vision was prepared for the nature it found in the American Southwest.

At the inauguration of President John F. Kennedy in 1961, poet Robert Frost read his poem "The Gift Outright," whose first line is "The land was ours before we were the land's." With his New Englander's sense of colonial history, Frost meant that Americans had lived upon their land for a long time before the land began to live within them, to influence them with its own character, its own possibilities and logic and spirit. From England Americans had brought with them English customs, tools, crops, clothes, architecture, and political institutions. They soon realized that many of these habits did not fit the New World very well and that new ideas worked better. Crops such as corn and potatoes, which Native Americans had been growing for millennia, worked better than many Old World crops. Monarchy, too, seemed unproductive on American soil. "She was our land," said Frost, "more than a hundred years before we were her people." Even the American Revolution did not make Americans the land's people, for that required generations of living and struggling and dying upon the land, of turning the land into human experience, into stories and songs, meanings and emotions. Frost ends his poem with a vision of the still unknown, unlived American West: "the land vaguely realizing westward, but still unstoried, artless, unenhanced."[1]

As the American nation expanded westward, it developed some strong stories about the land, mainly stories of conquering the land, but also the stories of Emerson, Thoreau, Whitman, and Muir, in which the land spoke of other realities, of deep time and beauty and spirit. Yet when Americans encountered the desert Southwest, no one was prepared for it. Its bare rock, its brown and lifeless expanses, its deep canyons, and its strange eroded shapes were too different from the rest of the American continent. The Southwest defied the experience of both pioneers and poets.

This failure of recognition began with the first Europeans to see the Grand Canyon. In 1540 Spanish conquistadores came upon the canyon and imagined that the Colorado River was a creek about six feet wide, when it is really about three hundred feet (ninety-one meters) wide. The Spanish also failed to recognize the canyon's value, for they were seeking only gold and empire.

American pioneers, too, failed to recognize the Southwest. They tried to settle the Southwest with the strategies that had worked back east. They placed as many cattle on an acre as they had in Texas, and they clear-cut forests as they had in Michigan, but they often ruined the land and condemned their children to despair and defeat. The first explorers who tried to run the Colorado River brought boats that were designed for eastern lakes, and they had great trouble—and some died. The first painters and poets to see the Southwest struggled in a different way: Niagara Falls and Yosemite might fit their European ideals of beauty, but the Grand Canyon and the desert Southwest did not. Architects tried to fill the Southwest with European-style buildings, until the land began to speak to them and suggest its own shapes. The first pioneers took possession of the land as an economic resource, but they were not yet possessed by the land, and thus they did not see the value of honoring the land as national parks.

As the contending American visions of nature—reverence and conquest—clashed over the Grand Canyon, both traditions experienced confusion. Americans struggled to adjust their focus to a new and strange land, to see it on its own terms. Quite a bit of the American history of the Southwest—its exploration history, pioneer history, cultural history, and environmental history—consists of variations of the same story, the story of Americans slowly learning to recognize and appreciate the Southwest.

This was especially true for the Grand Canyon. Even by the standards of southwestern landscapes, the canyon is an extreme, surrealistic place. Its size and shapes and colors are larger and stranger and more outrageous than those of other canyons. Its challenges for explorers, pioneers, painters, and park rangers were as large as the canyon itself. The canyon demanded that Americans rewrite the scripts they had been acting out on smaller stages.

This book is, first of all, a cultural history. It explores how Americans encountered the Grand Canyon through their national identity and dreams, scientific and cultural ideas, evolving values about the land, religious aspirations, and artistic creations. It begins with some scientific history, how humans discovered the canyon's geological story, and how the shapes of the land have dictated the shapes of its human history. It shows how for Native Americans, the canyon was a home and sacred. It offers a lot of American frontier history, with a cast of characters as colorful as anywhere. It includes political history: the advocates, opponents, events, and policy decisions that went into making and continually reshaping a national park. It includes environmental history: how ideas about land use—or nonuse—have evolved. It offers intellectual history: the artists, poets, writers, and architects who gave shapes to a strange new place.

The canyon's history was driven by some of the largest forces of American history. From its beginning, America was an odd mixture of idealism and greed, and these forces have contended against one another in one realm after another, one decade after another. When these cultural forces arrived at the Grand Canyon, they were acted out in the grandest of theaters.

Being a short history, this book cannot include every detail, every event and person, of Grand Canyon history, but a short history does have the advantage that it stays focused on the big picture. History books are usually arranged by the chronological order of events, and for the most part this book is also, beginning with the rocks and then the Native Americans who accounted for 98 percent of the canyon's human history. Euro-American explorers are followed by land exploiters, answered by growing conservation values. Yet this is also a book of themes, some of which deserve their own chapters and suggest their own order. The geology chapter includes some of the canyon's explorers and some of the first cultural reactions to the canyon. We will first meet John Wesley Powell in the geology chapter, follow him down the Colorado River in the chapter on exploration, and learn more about his boat designs and cultural perceptions in the chapter about the canyon as a place for adventure. The chapter on Native Americans completes their story until today, rather than the old habit of stringing out their story as a marginal detail of the American national story. We will meet John Muir in the chapter on the conservation movement and learn more about his perceptions in a chapter devoted to cultural reactions to the canyon. A chapter on architecture shows how Mary Colter blended Native American traditions with evolving American ideas of what national parks are for.

This book's largest theme, how Americans came to recognize their land and tried to fit themselves to it, recurs in many chapters and subjects, in exploration, exploitation, conservation, art, literature, architecture, and adventure. America's evolving cultural values run deeply through Grand Canyon history, but in the end, no dreams of any nation were as deep as the Grand Canyon

CHAPTER ONE

Geology

The Land Writes the Human Stories

Neil Armstrong took one small step, the first of about thirty thousand steps it took to get to the bottom of the Grand Canyon. It was March 1964, and the Apollo astronauts were taking their first steps to learn the geology they would need on the moon. There was no better geological training ground than the Grand Canyon, which offered Earth's best display of rock layers and geological forces.

The geologists in charge of training the astronauts in geology had selected the Grand Canyon for another reason. They wanted to persuade the astronauts that geology was a great adventure. Many astronauts had been reluctant to learn geology, for they were quite preoccupied with learning to fly complicated and dangerous spacecraft. If they crashed on the moon, it hardly mattered what the moon rocks were made of—they would be just as dead. By the end of their Grand Canyon hike, many of the astronauts had become enthralled with geology.

The astronauts hiked down the South Kaibab Trail, stayed overnight at Phantom Ranch, and hiked up the Bright Angel Trail the next day. They had received permission from the National Park Service (NPS) to use geology hammers to chip off rock samples; today's hikers can see little nicks in the cliffs made by the same hands that brought back rocks from the moon. The astronauts studied basic geological principles, such as how older rocks lay beneath younger rocks and how original strata could be disrupted by faulting. They learned how to read geology maps and compare aerial photographs with the landscape in front of them, a skill needed when approaching a lunar landing site. They learned the basics of Grand Canyon geology, how the black rocks at the bottom were 1.8 billion years old, about 40 percent of the age of Earth and about one-seventh the age of the universe. They learned how the Colorado River had carved through those rocks relatively recently, maybe 6 million years ago.

The astronauts were learning geology not just with their minds but with their bodies, which were registering the events of eons. The deep calm sea of 340 million years ago dictated where the cliffs were tallest and where the trail was steepest and where, on the hike back up, lungs and muscles would strain the hardest and feet would blister fastest. (Yes, even astronauts got blisters on canyon hikes.) The shallow seas of a half-billion years ago dictated where the hiking was easiest. The clash of tectonic plates tens of millions of years ago meant that the descent was a vertical mile and that the canyon rim held forests and mountain lions, while the bottom was a desert with cacti and rattlesnakes. Ancient faulting dictated the general route of the trails, and more recent erosion dictated every twist and grade. The astronauts were walking on the tracks of trilobites 515 million years old, imprinted in mud that had felt the stronger tides of a moon that had been closer to Earth.

For people who live on flat terrain, geology may seem an abstract idea, but for people who live in more rugged landscapes, geology defines not only their daily efforts but their entire history. This was truer for the Grand Canyon than for almost anywhere.

The uplift of the Colorado Plateau to 7,000 feet (2,133 m) or more meant that the canyon rims were cooler and moister than the surrounding deserts, allowing humans to survive there by hunting and farming. The uplift created faults that broke up the cliffs and left debris slopes down which game animals and humans could enter the canyon, and it created springs, creeks, rocks broken into soil, open spaces for farming, and a lot of rocks the right size for building houses. Sponges that lived in the seas of 270 million years ago became hard chert nodules that human hands shaped into tools and projectile points. Yet the canyon's ruggedness also meant that living there was rugged.

Geology dictated that the Colorado River was steep, swift, and choked with boulders swept down from side drainages, boulders that formed turbulent rapids. When explorer John Wesley Powell came down the Colorado River to study geology, he had to fight geology for his life. Quiet geological events of nearly 2 billion years ago dictate where today's river runners will worry, have sleepless nights, and sometimes die. Lava flows of nearly 1 million years ago mean that river runners feel the heat while scouting Lava Falls rapid.

Geology created the strata and colors and erosional shapes that humans decided were beautiful and that drew them from all over the world. The

Grand Canyon's geology spoke so powerfully that Native Americans saw their sacred origins, Christians saw the face of God, and poets and scientists saw primordial forces and mysteries.

Perhaps most important, geology defended the canyon against mining. The canyon held virtually no gold or silver. In the 1880s massive copper deposits were being discovered in southern Arizona, which made Arizona the world's leading copper producer (in the year 2010 Arizona was still producing a majority of the copper mined in the United States). This copper frenzy sent many prospectors into the Grand Canyon. If they had found major copper lodes in the canyon, which still lacked any legal protection, the canyon would have been helpless. It would have become a chain of huge open-pit mines and been streaked with mining talus. The cliffs would have been carved and tunneled for railroad tracks and roads to twist down to the mines. The canyon would have been filled with the smoke and noise of trains hauling out ore. Copper smelters on the rim would have poured smoke into the air and into the canyon, shrouding the view. The rim would have held massive piles of processed ore—or perhaps the ore would have been dumped back into the canyon. Perhaps instead of being powered by coal, the smelters would have been powered by spiderwebs of wires coming up from hydroelectric dams on the river, dams flooding dozens of miles of the canyon. The rim would have held smoke-dingy towns with shabby housing, rowdy bars, labor unrest, and company bullies.

None of this happened, thanks to geology. The canyon did hold some copper, but not enough to be very tempting. The canyon used its greatest strength, its geology, to defend itself against desecration.

When the Apollo astronauts reached the Colorado River, they may have imagined the ghost of John Wesley Powell passing down it. Powell's journey was as epic as a journey to the moon and required the same rare mixture of toughness, scientific intelligence, appetite for exploration, skill, and bravery. On July 20, 1869, exactly a century before Apollo 11 landed on the moon, Powell's expedition was upstream from the Grand Canyon, and in his diary for that day crew member George Bradley described the landscape as "wild desolation," close to Buzz Aldrin's description of the moon as "magnificent desolation." The astronauts knew more about the moon before going there than Powell knew about the Grand Canyon. Powell was gambling his life on one then controversial theory of geology.

In 1830, four years before Powell was born, English geologist Charles

Lyell published *Principles of Geology,* and in 1872, as Powell finished his second expedition down the Colorado River, Lyell published his eleventh updated edition of *Principles.* Lyell developed an idea called uniformitarianism, which held that the world's landscapes were shaped by the same geological forces we see at work today: rainfall, frost, streams and rivers, erosion, sedimentation, volcanic flows, and earthquakes. Everything happened gradually: sediments built up in the ocean and turned into rock, the earth was uplifted, and water eroded the land grain by grain into valleys and canyons, carrying new sediments to the ocean to begin the cycle anew. For mere raindrops to create canyons, it took enormous amounts of time.

Lyell was challenging the prevailing view of geology, catastrophism, which held that the land was shaped by violent events. In catastrophism entire mountain ranges might be created by one massive earthquake and eroded significantly by one massive flood. Catastrophism did not require an ancient Earth; it viewed today's world as the quiet aftermath of a far more dramatic epoch, and it seemed to have a biblical sensibility in the spirit of Noah's flood. When applied to the Grand Canyon, catastrophism might say that the canyon was created when a massive earthquake split the earth, and then water found this fissure and formed the Colorado River; uniformitarianism held that the Colorado River and thunderstorms carved the canyon over eons of time. The year before Powell launched his river expedition, Britain's leading physicist, William Thomson, Lord Kelvin, launched a major attack against uniformitarianism, saying that his calculations of the rate at which Earth had cooled from its molten beginning gave an age of around one hundred million years, not nearly enough time for sedimentation and erosion to have created today's world. Clarence King, the first director of the US Geological Survey, was scornful of uniformitarianism.

As a young man John Wesley Powell took an avid interest in natural history, and he became convinced of the truth of uniformitarianism. His college education was sporadic, and in geology he was largely self-taught, including studying the fossils he unearthed at Vicksburg as a Union officer in charge of digging earthworks. After the Civil War he taught geology and other natural sciences at Illinois Wesleyan College. Powell was fascinated by the report of John Strong Newberry, who in 1858 became the first geologist to examine the Grand Canyon. Newberry declared that the canyon offered the world's best exposure of rock strata, and he emphasized that it was "*wholly due to the action of water.* Probably nowhere in the world has the action of this agent produced results so surprising, both as regards their magnitude and their peculiar character."[1]

Newberry had struggled terribly to get only glimpses of the western end of the canyon; Powell saw that the best way to survey the whole canyon was by boat. Yet as Powell began dreaming of a river expedition, he was warned that the Colorado might hold waterfalls like Niagara or flow underground for miles at a stretch. Powell might come to an impassable waterfall, be unable to row upstream against the current, be unable to scale the cliffs to escape, and starve in the desert. Powell reasoned that if a powerful river like the Colorado had been carving the canyon for eons, it would have carved away major obstacles and evened out its descent. If uniformitarianism was true, it implied a relatively uniform river. As a geologist Powell was hardly infallible. As he entered the Grand Canyon, he mistook limestone cliffs for marble and named the canyon's first section "Marble Canyon," a terrible omen for someone who was gambling his life on his knowledge of geology. All the way down the river, Powell and his men worried about coming upon an impassable waterfall. Yet Powell's faith in uniformitarianism proved true, more or less. The river held hundreds of difficult rapids, and the expedition turned into a life-and-death struggle, but they made it.

In the often poetic book Powell wrote about his expedition, he emphasized the canyon's geology: "All about me are interesting geologic records. The book is open and I can read as I run." At a time when even Charles Lyell was still hesitant to declare that all valleys were carved by rivers, Powell defined the canyon as a uniformitarian reality: "The carving of the Grand Canyon is the work of rains and rivers. . . . We think of the mountains as forming clouds about their brows, but the clouds have formed the mountains. Great continental blocks are upheaved from beneath the sea by internal geologic forces that fashion the earth. Then the wandering clouds, the tempest-bearing clouds, the rainbow-decked clouds, with mighty power and with wonderful skill, carve out valleys and canyons and fashion hills and cliffs and mountains. The clouds are the artists sublime."[2] Powell returned for another river expedition in 1871–72 and then land surveys, and when he became the second director of the US Geological Survey in 1881 he sent his protégés to the canyon. (We will discuss the Powell expedition further in chapter 3.)

One of Powell's protégés, Charles Walcott, also self-educated in geology,

FIGURE 1.1. Inspired by his love of geology, John Wesley Powell led river expeditions through the Grand Canyon in 1869 and 1871–72. Engraving by R. A. Muller.

became one of the world's great paleontologists. In 1909 Walcott (by then the head of the Smithsonian Institution) discovered the Burgess Shale in the Canadian Rockies, a mother lode of fossils, from which Walcott excavated sixty-five thousand specimens. Burgess Shale fossils illustrated "the Cambrian Explosion" about five hundred million years ago, in which life, after remaining one-celled for more than three billion years, shows up in most of the complex forms seen today. Before Walcott found the Burgess Shale, he had seen the Cambrian Explosion inside the Grand Canyon.

In 1882 Powell improved an old Indian route into the canyon, today's Nankoweap Trail. Powell sent Walcott to spend seventy-two freezing winter days at the canyon bottom, to study the rock layers Powell had passed too hurriedly on his river trip. As the river descended, Powell had seen rock layer after layer emerging from underground. The Nankoweap Trail arrived at the river where the Bright Angel Shale was exposed, nearly the lowest layer of the canyon's main sequence of sedimentary rocks. The Bright Angel Shale had been formed at about the same time as the Burgess Shale, from the same process of mud and silt accumulating off the edge of the North American continent. This mud was perfect for creating fossils; the Bright Angel Shale is even loaded with the tracks of trilobites. As Walcott went downstream into Precambrian rocks, he discovered fossilized stromatolites, sponge-like colonies of cyanobacteria; this was the first discovery of preserved Precambrian cells. The canyon's rock library held a rich record of life's evolution.

Three years previously, Walcott had connected the canyon's rock record with the rest of the Colorado Plateau. He had surveyed a line 80 miles long, from the bottom of the Grand Canyon, up Kanab Creek, to Bryce Canyon. The elevation change was about 8,000 feet (2,438 m), but because this included tilted cliffs, he was mapping out geological layers totaling 13,000 feet (3,962 m), or 2.5 miles (4 km), loaded with five hundred million years of fossils, of which Walcott collected twenty-five hundred. Such a geological and paleontological cross-section was possible nowhere else on Earth. In his Washington career Walcott became a trusted adviser to President Teddy Roosevelt and encouraged his conservation agenda, including protecting the Grand Canyon.

A few years after Walcott mapped the canyon's geological layers, biologist C. Hart Merriam mapped its ecological layers. Merriam traveled from the 12,600-foot (3,840-m) top of the San Francisco Peaks near Flagstaff to the bottom of the Grand Canyon, a 10,000-foot (3,048-m) difference. He observed huge changes of vegetation and wildlife, which he called "life zones," like going from the Arctic to Mexico. As with geology, the canyon was helping to define the science of ecology.

Another Powell protégé, Clarence Dutton, was also self-educated in geology and shared Powell's ability to write poetically. At Yale Dutton studied for the ministry, but the Civil War led him into the Army Ordnance Corps, which remained his career, though he received generous time off

FIGURE 1.2. Architect Mary Colter's geological fireplace (inside her Bright Angel Lodge), made with rocks from every strata inside the canyon.

to join surveys of the West. In 1882 Dutton published a report, *Tertiary History of the Grand Cañon Region,* which was mainly a scientific discussion of landscapes and geology but today is admired for its humanistic response to the canyon, for helping to define how we should see it. Dutton also gave names to many canyon landmarks.

The first explorers and settlers of the American frontier had the chance to give names to the landscape. As John Wesley Powell came down the Colorado River, he gave many descriptive names, such as Flaming Gorge, Whirlpool Canyon, and Labyrinth Canyon. Of course, the land had already held names for centuries, Native American names that often contained poetry and sacred meanings. Americans adopted some of these names, often without even knowing what they meant. More often, Americans began rebranding the continent with names from their own history, first the names of European kings and cities and then the names of American presidents, heroes, and railroad executives. Thousands of places got named for the first pioneer to settle there or die there or for some minor event. A mesa that had been a sacred conduit between Native Americans and their gods might become "Horse Thief Mesa." If landscapes were being named in today's era of corporate sponsorships, the Grand Canyon might hold "Coca-Cola Mesa."

Clarence Dutton's theologically trained imagination ranged higher. For him, only the names of gods could do justice to the canyon's grandeur. To inner-canyon buttes he gave names such as Vishnu Temple and Zoroaster Temple. Dutton was following a well-established romantic tradition of seeing architectural shapes and mythological motifs in landscapes, but he applied it to the Grand Canyon with greater dignity than the often more fanciful uses elsewhere. Subsequent geologists, geographers, and writers followed Dutton's lead and designated additional religious names, so today the canyon holds clusters of landmarks named for the gods and heroes of the Egyptians (such as Cheops Pyramid), Greeks, Romans, Buddhists, Hindus, Germans, and the Old Testament.

Ironically, Americans awarded almost no names from the Hopis and Zunis, for whom the canyon truly was their sacred place of creation. At least Dutton gave the canyon the dignity of being a sacred space, a place for reverence before the powers of creation, however people defined those powers. Dutton did correctly identify the primary response that many future visitors would feel to the canyon. Yet he was also introducing invasive species of ideas, imposing images from non-American civilizations onto a land where they had no connection. In the decades to come, some writers would object to Dutton's approach. John C. Van Dyke scoffed that "the parlor-car poet was abroad in the land and in consequence the mock-heroic and the absurd have been put upon the map." Mary Austin complained about "the silly names cut out of a mythological dictionary and shaken in a hat before they were applied to the Grand Cañon for the amazing number of Americans who can never see anything unless it is supposed to look like something else."[3] Nature writers Van Dyke and Austin were committed to seeing the desert Southwest on its own terms, and they favored giving Grand Canyon landmarks Native American names. In 1916 Aldo Leopold (who three decades later would join Van Dyke and Austin as a major nature writer) was working for the US Forest Service, which still managed the Grand Canyon, and he drew up a master plan and proposed abolishing Dutton's nomenclature and replacing it with the original Native American names. But it was too late: Dutton's names were already on the map.

In addition to proclaiming the canyon to be a sacred space, Dutton astutely identified a big problem with how people would experience the canyon, a problem that would preoccupy the first generation of artists, writers, and tourists to see it. The canyon did not fit the ideas about natural beauty that Americans had inherited from Europe. Natural beauty was supposed to be a living land, "England's green and pleasant land," Eden-like, with trees, flowers, rolling pastures, life-giving streams and lakes, and with shepherds (and maybe ruins) that identified it as a home for humans. It is even possible that such images of good landscapes were biologically programmed when humans evolved on green savannas with plentiful trees and water holes. Most of America had fitted this pastoral image. The desert Southwest came as a shock. The desert held little green or blue, but mostly naked rock and dirt with weird shapes and garish colors. The desert's heat, dryness, and physical barriers were hostile to human presence or use. Yet Dutton perceived that the desert and its canyons would in time come to be appreciated on their own terms:

> The Grand Cañon of the Colorado is a great innovation in modern ideas of scenery, and in our conceptions of the grandeur, beauty, and power of nature. . . . It must be dwelt upon and studied, and the study must comprise the slow acquisition of the meaning and spirit of that marvelous scenery. . . . The lover of nature, whose perceptions have been trained in the Alps, in Italy, Germany, or New England . . . in Scotland or Colorado, would enter this strange region with a shock, and dwell there for a time with a sense of oppression, and perhaps with horror. Whatsoever things he had learned to regard as beautiful and noble he would seldom or never see. . . . Whatsoever might be bold and striking would at first seem only grotesque. The colors would be the very ones he had learned to shun as tawdry and bizarre. . . . But time would bring a gradual change. Someday he would suddenly become conscious that outlines which at first seemed harsh and trivial have grace and meaning; that forms which seemed grotesque are full of dignity.[4]

Dutton was right that many early visitors to the canyon would see it with a sense of oppression, even horror. Dutton's solution was to bypass traditional images of scenic beauty and rely on the idea of the sublime, which allowed for more chaos in a landscape. The sublime, which had a long pedigree in philosophy and romanticism, involved landscapes that were far larger and more powerful than humans, against which humans would feel their smallness, especially their smallness before God. Romantic art and poetry were rich with images of humans dwarfed by gloomy Alpine chasms, a good fit for the chasms of the American Southwest. Dutton gave the name "Point Sublime" to his favorite Grand Canyon–rim viewpoint, and he repeatedly used the word *sublime* for the canyon.

Two decades after Dutton wrote the words quoted above, John C. Van Dyke and Mary Austin, after years of living in the Mojave Desert, took up Dutton's challenge and wrote books that sought to redefine the desert as a beautiful and powerful landscape; Van Dyke's *The Desert* was published in 1901, Austin's *Land of Little Rain* in 1903. Yet instead of trying to give meaning to desert landscapes by giving them mythological and architectural images, they insisted that the desert's own stories were sufficient.

For John C. Van Dyke, the desert's genuine power lay in its ancient geological forces, beside which human lives were tiny, fleeting mysteries. In his 1920 book, *The Grand Canyon of the Colorado,* he wrote:

> The pyramid of Cheops was the labor of thousands of slaves over many years. . . . But here at the Canyon the so-called Cheops Pyramid was the labor of Nature over thousands of centuries. . . . Perhaps the first marauder who broke into the tomb in the heart of the Gizeh Pyramid was brought to a standstill by seeing in the dust of the floor a naked footprint—the footprint of the last attendant who had gone out and sealed the door behind him five thousand years before; but here in the under-strata of the Canyon Pyramid are the sand-ripples left by the waves of a primal sea perhaps five million years ago. You can almost see to a nicety just where the last wave broke. These are the footprints of Creation, beside which those of the human seem so small and so inconsequential.[5]

This nugget of geological poetry was more vivid than anything in Dutton's book, which dealt mainly with aesthetic appearances. Van Dyke, a Rutgers University art history professor who had written books about aesthetics, did not rely on the sublime or aesthetics to justify why desert landscapes held power and deserved appreciation, though Van Dyke would also make his case for the canyon being beautiful.

In 1902, the year in between the publication of Van Dyke's and Austin's books of desert appreciation, John Muir came to the Grand Canyon. Muir's sense of nature had been defined in the Sierra Nevada, with its waterfalls, giant trees, and lush meadows, and true to Dutton's prediction John

Muir struggled with the canyon's desert bleakness. To his editor at *Century Illustrated Monthly Magazine*, who wanted a Grand Canyon article from Muir, Muir confesséd that this was "the toughest job I ever tackled." Muir fumbled around with the architectural similes that Van Dyke, Austin, and Leopold disdained, and he could not find much affection for desert vegetation, but he soon decided that the canyon's main power was geological. In Yosemite Muir had developed a strong eye for geology, but Yosemite was all about glacial erosion, whereas the Grand Canyon offered a testament about creation. Perhaps taking the book metaphor from Powell, Muir saw "a grand geological library, a collection of stone books.... And with what wonderful scriptures are their pages filled—myriad forms of successive floras and faunas, lavishly illustrated with colored drawings, carrying us back into the midst of the life of a past infinitely remote. And as we go on and on, studying this old, old life in the light of the life beating warmly about us, we enrich and lengthen our own."[6]

Seven years later Muir returned to the canyon with John Burroughs, who had been America's leading nature writer for forty years. Burroughs's eye had been trained in the Catskill Mountains, and he too worked to adjust his vision to the canyon. He too decided that the canyon's primary power was geological. Writers loved the book metaphor: "The book of earthly revelation, as shown by the great science, lies wide open in that land, as it does in few other places on the globe. Its leaves fairly flutter in the wind, and the print is so large.... Not being able to read it at all, or not taking any interest in it, is like going to Rome or Egypt or Jerusalem, knowing nothing of the history of those lands."[7]

Muir and Burroughs also followed the lead of Clarence Dutton in accepting that naked rock had a beauty of its own. In the decades to come, this perception grew until visitors came to the Grand Canyon expecting to find a supreme expression of natural beauty. When Buzz Aldrin described the lunar desert as "magnificent desolation" and not George Bradley's "wild desolation," he was combining two once incompatible words that had been melded together by visionaries like Dutton, Muir, Austin, and Van Dyke. Aldrin's companion Neil Armstrong had a similar reaction to the lunar surface: "It has a stark beauty all its own. It's like much of the high desert of the United States. It's different, but it's very pretty out here."[8] In saying "the high desert," Armstrong may have been thinking of his time at the Grand Canyon.

FIGURE 1.3. John Muir (*top*) and John Burroughs (*third from top*) on Bright Angel Trail in 1909. They helped define the Grand Canyon as, first of all, a geological experience.

The canyon and the moon also shared a stubborn mystery: their origin. Even after astronauts had returned from the moon with rocks loaded with clues, and even after the world's smartest geologists had studied the Grand Canyon for a century and a half, geologists were still trying to figure out how both were born. Both origins were complicated and unlikely events, and many clues had been erased. The canyon's origin was entangled in some of the central mysteries of geology, such as how the seafloor could be uplifted thousands of feet.

On his river expedition John Wesley Powell watched the Colorado River breaking one of the basic laws of rivers: rivers are supposed to flow from high ground to low ground. Yet the river carried Powell's boats straight into and through the Kaibab Upwarp, which rises thousands of feet to form the 7,000–8,000 foot (2,133–2,438-m) rims of the Grand Canyon. Puzzling over this, Powell theorized that the river had been entrenched in its course first and then the land rose around it, like a cake being lifted around a knife. Powell and other geologists had only vague ideas about why the land might rise; the theory of plate tectonics was still four decades from being proposed and a century from being accepted.

Plate tectonics theory created all sorts of connections between seemingly disparate landscapes and events; it explained how colliding plates lifted and folded the land, creating mountain ranges, volcanoes, and earthquakes. It explained how rocks deposited in the ocean could rise to become the Colorado Plateau—the "Four Corners" region made of brightly colored sedimentary rocks that erode into all sorts of exotic shapes, including arches, spires, hoodoos, mesas, and numerous canyons. It connected California earthquakes with the creation of the Grand Canyon, which happened relatively fast when the San Andreas Fault broke off the Baja Peninsula from the rest of Mexico and broke open the Gulf of California, giving the Colorado River access to the sea, greatly increasing the river's gradient and carving power.

Powell's theory of the river's "antecedence" gradually gave way to a far more complicated picture of a landscape that was originally tilted in the opposite direction than today's, with a different system of rivers. As this landscape was eroded away in some places and uplifted in other places, its rivers continued rearranging themselves. Several ancestral rivers combined to form today's Colorado River. This most likely occurred through "headward erosion," in which the lower Colorado ate its way upward from the Gulf of California and committed "stream piracy" by capturing other rivers. This happened relatively quickly in geological terms, within the last 6 million years. Geological "species" like rivers and canyons evolve just like biological species. In this respect, the Grand Canyon is very unlike the dormant moon: it is a living entity with a river for a beating heart. Powell had felt his own heart racing to that ancient heartbeat, and his heart had told him that humans, even the bravest, were very small creatures compared with rivers and canyons.

When the Santa Fe Railway began bringing tourists to the Grand Canyon in 1901, scientists were still accepting Lord Kelvin's estimate that Earth was somewhere around 100 million years old. But things changed fast, as science discovered X-rays in 1895 and explored radioactivity, which offered a new energy source for driving geological events and a new method for dating rocks—first done in 1907. Earth's age ballooned fifty times, to 4.6 billion years. Humans watched themselves being dwarfed by time, inhuman forces, and a long parade of strange species. The lonely expanses of the scientific cosmos gave humans an identity crisis that would occupy much of the intellectual, cultural, and religious energy of the twentieth century.

In the Grand Canyon this identity confusion was symbolized by Charles Walcott finding the Cambrian Explosion in the rock layer with the most prominent Christian name in the canyon: Bright Angel. John Wesley Powell had taken "Bright Angel" from a Methodist hymn and given it to a sparkling creek; today it's also the name of a side canyon, geological fault, trail, lodge, and other things. The canyon also contains a section named in honor of the founders of evolutionary theory: Darwin Plateau, Wallace Butte, and Huxley Terrace. These, plus Evolution Amphitheater, are right across the river from Holy Grail Temple, named for the Last Supper chalice.

This mix-up of names was reflected in the mixed feelings of many people gazing into the canyon, where geological time and power went from being abstractions to being palpable. Feeling a tension between science and faith, many Christians expanded their concept of God to include billions of years and a much greater creation story, while others tried to shrink the geological story into the framework of a seven-day creation and Noah's flood. Other people adopted a largely scientific worldview. For John Wesley Powell, the idea of evolution was full of hope; it was a cosmic endorsement of human progress, not just biological, scientific, and technological progress but moral progress. Powell's personal story embodied the intellectual changes of his era. His Methodist minister father had named him for the founder of Methodism, John Wesley, in hope that John would become a minister. But Powell's father had grown up in the same English town, at the same time, as Charles Darwin, and Darwin's vision of an ancient, creative nature would fire John's imagination and lead him into a scientific career.

Other people viewed the geological and evolutionary story with regret. At the beginning of the twentieth century, Edgar Lee Masters was the law partner of Clarence Darrow, who in the Scopes Trial of 1925 defended the idea of evolution. Masters became a famous poet with his *Spoon River Anthology*, and in 1935 he wrote a poem called "The Grand Canyon" in which he gazed into the canyon and accepted its evidence for evolution yet also yearned to see some sort of divine presence. As we will see in chapter 6, other cultural leaders would use the Grand Canyon to try to figure out the human meanings of the new scientific story.

CHAPTER TWO

Native Americans
The Canyon as Home

Geologists were not the first people to look into the Grand Canyon and see the powers of creation and the emergence of life and humans. Native Americans had seen this long ago. For two prominent tribes, the Hopis and the Zunis, the Grand Canyon is the sacred place where they emerged into this world from a series of underworlds. For them, the canyon was not "the West," defined by the direction of American history; it was the center and the source.

The Hopis and Zunis are the descendants of the Ancestral Puebloan people who a thousand years ago built an elaborate society in the Southwest, including famous centers like Chaco Canyon and Mesa Verde. The Ancestral Puebloans (often called Anasazi) did an unlikely and brave thing: they developed an agricultural society in a desert. Perhaps all farmers appreciate the rains and soil more than do urban peoples, but the challenges of farming in an arid region gave the Ancestral Puebloans an especially acute appreciation of the generative powers of the land, seeds, and rain. In their creation story, humans emerged from the nurturing earth. Whereas Christian churches point toward the sky, Puebloan "churches," or kivas, are chambers embedded in the earth. It seems natural that the Puebloans would feel affinity with the deepest of all chambers in the earth, the Grand Canyon. The canyon's power was magnified further by its holding the Colorado River, the largest, most powerful body of water the Ancestral Puebloans would ever see.

At the bottom of the canyon, the Hopis and Zunis identify unusual geological structures as their places of emergence. For the Hopis, it is the Sipapuni, a kiva-like mineral dome in the gorge of the Little Colorado River, a few miles from the Colorado River. For the Zunis, it is Ribbon Falls, a waterfall and mineral dome on Bright Angel Creek, a few miles from the Colorado River. Both domes were created by water, the Sipapuni by a

spring welling up from within and the dome at Ribbon Falls by the waterfall from above. Both domes are strange looking, strange enough to invoke
the mystery of creation, the mystery of order emerging out of chaos. In geological terms the domes are made of dissolved limestone, limestone made
from the bodies of ancient sea creatures, the bodies and eons from which
human life did indeed emerge. Agricultural peoples all over the world have
creation stories in which humans emerged from the earth, just like their
crops, but in adding the Grand Canyon to that image the Hopis and Zunis
created the world's most powerful expression of it.

The Hopis and Zunis knew about the Sipapuni and Ribbon Falls because
their ancestors, or at least a small portion of them, lived at the bottom and
on the rim of the Grand Canyon a thousand years ago. This was at the peak
of Ancestral Puebloan society, when a somewhat more generous climate
encouraged them to expand their settlements to many new areas. When
a drought then made farming at the canyon much harder, the Puebloans
left and migrated to places with reliable water sources. In their new villages the Grand Canyon Puebloans joined people who were migrating in
from other areas, and together they became the Hopi and Zuni peoples.
The canyon Puebloans told their stories about the Grand Canyon, and the
canyon held such power for the human imagination that even Hopis and
Zunis who had never seen the Grand Canyon accepted it as their place of
emergence.

One of the Hopis' central stories is about Tiyo, a youth who went on a
quest down the Colorado River. Tiyo sealed himself inside a hollow log,
endured the rapids of the Grand Canyon, and arrived at the home of the
Snake People, who knew the secrets of bringing rain. Tiyo carried this
knowledge back to the Hopis, who enact it in their snake dance.

For centuries, the Hopis made a difficult pilgrimage back to the canyon
and the Sipapuni, performed ceremonies along the way, and gathered salt
from a deposit along the Colorado River. The Hopis could have obtained
higher-quality salt from a much easier pilgrimage, but the salt's primary
spiritual value came from its Grand Canyon origin. For the Hopis, the
Sipapuni is also where the spirits of the dead enter the next world. Hopi
kivas hold a symbolic Sipapuni, a hole in the ground that reminds them of
their origin in the Grand Canyon.

The Zunis are now making a pilgrimage to Ribbon Falls, as part of their
raft trips through the canyon. From the river they hike six miles, carrying

FIGURE 2.1. Hopi artist Fred Kabotie painting murals, inside Desert View Watchtower, depicting the story of Tiyo's journey through the Grand Canyon.

ammo cans full of prayer feathers. Ammo cans are surplus army gear, once used for storing ammunition, now used by river runners to keep their supplies dry—the Zunis have turned an instrument of war into an instrument for giving blessings.

The Ancestral Puebloans farmed at the Grand Canyon for about two hundred years, but this was a relatively brief anomaly in the canyon's long human history, in which humans survived by hunting and gathering. The oldest human artifact found at the canyon is a broken Clovis point, about twelve thousand years old. Clovis points were used by hunters at the end of the Ice Age, when large game animals such as mammoths required large spear points. This twelve-thousand-year date corresponds roughly with the dates of the oldest artifacts found in many other areas of the Southwest. It is likely that humans arrived at the Grand Canyon before twelve thousand years ago, but their traces are hard to find—that Clovis point was discovered by a bird-watcher wandering in the woods. It is a safe guess the first humans to discover the Grand Canyon were awed by it.

There were good reasons for hunter-gatherers—whom archaeologists call the Archaic Culture—to remain at the Grand Canyon. The river and the forest vegetation on the rims were draws for game animals, and the canyon's range of elevations and ecosystems offered a greater variety of wild plants in a shorter space than other landscapes. Humans seem to have continued living at the canyon through the millennia, but in small numbers— it takes a large area to support a small group of hunter-gatherers. Their projectile points continued shrinking in size and changing in design as Ice Age animals died out, which left deer and bighorn sheep the largest game animals, and as, much later, spears were replaced by the bow and arrow, which allowed smaller points to make larger impacts.

The Archaic Culture left us a few clues about their religious life. Inside the canyon they left hundreds of figurines made out of willow twigs, shaped like deer or bighorn sheep, many with a sharp twig penetrating them, like a hunter's spear. Most of these figurines were left in caves, often high up on canyon cliffs, hard to access, caves with no evidence of human habitation. It is unlikely these figurines were toys or decorations, more likely they were offerings in rituals that encouraged a successful hunt. The same hands that wove these willow figurines also painted many murals under canyon overhangs. One of the most elaborate murals, called Shamans Gallery, is full of enigmatic spirit-like beings. This too may have been a place for rituals or visions or healing.

Yet the hunting-gathering way of life could be very challenging, especially in a difficult landscape like the Grand Canyon. All over earth, whenever humans saw the possibility and advantages of surviving through farming, they gave up hunting and gathering, at least as their primary food source—they may have continued hunting and gathering on the side or seasonally. Farming offered a far more concentrated source of plant nutrition than had wild plants, and it was far more predictable than hunting. Farming allowed people to accumulate a large surplus of food to get them through winters or drought years and to maintain domesticated animals. Farming allowed people to stay in the same place, to build stone houses and accumulate possessions, and to develop specialized skills such as pottery making. Farming could support a much larger population.

At the Grand Canyon farming began with the arrival of corn. Corn had been grown in Mexico for thousands of years, where slowly it was bred for higher yields and more arid conditions. Corn gradually spread northward, and by about three thousand years ago it began showing up at the canyon. People were cautious about giving up a long-proven survival strategy for something new, so planting crops only gradually supplanted hunting and gathering. A new culture evolved, the Basketmakers, who did not yet possess pottery. They began building villages. Their homes were pithouses, dug partly into the ground (which offered better temperature control) and finished with logs aboveground, with a ladder entrance through the roof—a design that evolved into the kiva. The Basketmakers also began growing cotton and weaving it into clothing much more comfortable and artistic than the buckskin worn by the Archaic people. About seventeen hundred years ago the Basketmakers began making pottery, useful for protecting grain and seeds against rodents and insects and for carrying and storing water. By about twelve hundred years ago, the Basketmakers had developed into a full-fledged agricultural society, the Ancestral Puebloans.

The Colorado River is an anomaly among the world's great rivers: it is a massive river flowing through a desert, carrying water that originated far away, bound for an ocean far away. In this the Colorado is like the Nile and the Tigris-Euphrates. While the Archaic people were barely surviving along the Colorado River, great agricultural civilizations were arising along the Nile and the Tigris-Euphrates, stimulated by the need to organize large-scale irrigation projects. With the Ancestral Puebloans the Colorado River too now had an agricultural civilization, and its ruins, its Chaco and Mesa Verde, would join the Egyptian pyramids in fascinating the future. Yet the Colorado River was far less favorable for agriculture and civilization. Most of the Colorado River was locked inside deep canyons, leaving only scattered and small fans of soil for farming. The steep gradient of the Colorado River and its landscapes made farmers pay a steep price in erosion. Chaco and Mesa Verde would arise on distant tributaries of the Colorado River, on lands more open and less rocky. This great river would not be the center of civilization, but the periphery. For the Ancestral Puebloans who lived at the Grand Canyon, their agricultural opportunities were poorer, their travel was much harder, and their population and villages were smaller. Still, they found and filled every habitable nook of the canyon, building a long network of settlements.

The rise of Ancestral Puebloan society was encouraged by an improvement in the climate and rainfall, a relatively small improvement, but in a marginal climate like the desert Southwest a modest improvement made a

FIGURE 2.2. Ancestral Puebloan ruins on the Colorado River, near the mouth of Bright Angel Creek. In the background is the bridge on South Kaibab Trail, used by hikers and mules, and the boat beach used by river runners.

big difference. It meant that springs flowed more reliably and that the soil retained more moisture.

At the canyon the Ancestral Puebloans tested out every patch of land that was wide enough and wet enough to support farming. On the canyon floor they preferred side canyons or creek deltas that offered reliable springs and streams, such as Bright Angel or Nankoweap, but they also did well in drainages with intermittent flows, such as Unkar. They constructed check dams and ditches and terraces to make the most of the water supply. Though they were living beside a mighty river, they needed rain, for the steep gradient between river and crops would not allow irrigation canals and the effort required to carry huge amounts of water from river to crops would have taken more energy than the crops would give back. At least the gradient offered some protection from the river, whose spring-flood rampages could wipe out a village and a year's crops.

Higher up in the canyon, on terraces such as the Tonto Platform, springs and creeks supported farming at places like Indian Garden. On the canyon rims a mixture of spring snowmelt and summer rains allowed farming in extensive areas. On the North Rim snowfalls of two hundred inches, still melting in June, offered a generous, time-released water supply, if a short growing season. Some canyon residents made seasonal migrations from the rim to the river. In the summer they farmed at Walhalla Glades on the North Rim or in the Desert View area on the South Rim, and in the winter they farmed at Unkar or on other large side-canyon deltas in the canyon below. Growing two crops in two climates minimized the risk of losing a crop to bad weather. People also traveled for social and trading purposes. Even inside the canyon, where settlements were separated by miles of steep topography, neighbors—often relatives—wore trails for visiting one another.

Settlements were small, with a dozen or two dozen people, often one or two extended families. Villages consisted of a few houses or a communal pueblo with a dozen rooms; almost all buildings were one story, made of stones and mortar and wood beams, constructed with considerable skill. A few famous ruins such as Mesa Verde have created a popular image of the Ancestral Puebloans as cliff dwellers, with homes tucked into cliffs reachable only by ladder, but in fact most Ancestral Puebloan villages were out in the open, close to their fields, often on hilltops or ridgelines that offered summer breezes and better views. The canyon Ancestral Puebloans did use the cliffs to build granaries to store their crops and seeds.

Corn remained the mainstay of the Ancestral Puebloan diet; it was much smaller than the corn that comes out of Iowa today, but it was also tougher, able to grow in poorer conditions. Along with corn, the Ancestral Puebloans relied on beans and squash. Together, corn, beans, and squash provided most of the nutrients needed by the human body, and they also offered good crop rotation so that the soil would not be depleted. To supplement these crops, the Ancestral Puebloans gathered wild plants such as prickly-pear cactus and pinyon nuts and hunted rabbits and deer. The variety of foods available between the rim and the river offered a more balanced diet than that of many other Ancestral Puebloans. Yet chasing deer and gathering plants in the canyon's rugged terrain must have resulted in falls, broken bones, disabilities, and deaths.

The Ancestral Puebloans were not a homogeneous people across their whole territory, which stretched about five hundred miles; they were a culture that shared a way of life and common designs in architecture and pottery. But between regions there were still noticeable differences in architecture and pottery and probably in language and social organization. Today's Puebloans speak a variety of languages, some of them similar, but others, like Hopi and Zuni, quite different. The Chacoans had much more social hierarchy than the small, scattered pueblos of the Grand Canyon region. Archaeologists divide the Ancestral Puebloans into a half-dozen traditions. Three of these traditions lived at the Grand Canyon, blurring together where they met: the Kayenta and Virgin traditions on the north side of the Colorado River and the Kayenta and the Cohonina on the south side.

The Puebloan groups at the Grand Canyon traded goods between one another and with neighboring cultures. Trade goods arrived at the canyon from remarkable distances. There were beads made out of shells from the Pacific Ocean and from the Gulf of California, macaw feathers from Mexico, and pottery from the San Juan River basin in Utah. Grand Canyon Puebloans did have some high-quality items to trade to outsiders. They had hematite—used to make red paint for pottery and rock art—from a hematite mine inside the canyon, they had salt leaching out of ancient saltwater-formed rocks that did not crop out elsewhere, and they had obsidian, the best mineral for projectile points, from a mountain fifty miles south of the canyon. And they had the Grand Canyon: it is plausible that a few prehistoric tourists traveled to the canyon just to look at it.

With the emergence of an agricultural society came a different religious cosmology. For hunter-gatherers, the world is a very unpredictable place, with no permanent home, prey that could turn and attack, and plants and springs that might not appear where they were last year. This chaos is reflected in a cosmology full of powerful evil spirits that need to be constantly placated with magic. For farmers, the universe holds a far more reliable order. The cosmos is designed to sustain human life, with order-rich seeds that unfold in predictable ways, an earth that is nurturing, rains that come at the right season, and earth cycles that are connected with the powerful cycles of the night sky. For hunter-gatherers, human survival requires fighting the chaos of the cosmos, whereas for Puebloans survival requires obeying the order of the cosmos. The Puebloans developed an elaborate ceremonial cycle in which the spirits who control the cosmos make friendly visits to their villages, bringing the gifts of life.

Yet the desert Southwest was not the easiest place in which to trust in an orderly and nurturing cosmos. The rains and water sources varied considerably from year to year. The soils went dry and blew away too easily. Humans were always vulnerable.

About nine hundred years ago the Southwest's climate began disintegrating. The climate did not just revert to its former drier regime: it dropped into a decades-long drought. After centuries of expanding their population and building cities, the Ancestral Puebloans saw a void open up beneath them. Even Chaco Canyon, supported by the population and resources of a large region, struggled and failed and was abandoned. For little clusters of farmers at the Grand Canyon, who had always relied on themselves, there had never been much safety margin. The most marginal settlements soon failed, and the people left, perhaps joining relatives in better locations, but then those villages began failing. There was hunger, social chaos, and probably raiding and violence and religious angst— the gods were failing or punishing them. People streamed away from the canyon. After a half century of chaos, the final pueblo at the canyon was built, Tusayan on the South Rim, in the year AD 1185. It would endure for another quarter century, and then its people too would abandon the canyon.

The canyon's people would not forget the canyon and the awe they had felt for it. Nor would they forget the disaster that had ruined their society. The Puebloans would continue celebrating the nurturing earth and summoning the rain, but they would do so with an extra intensity born from an acute sense of vulnerability. This sense of vulnerability would mark a huge contrast with the Euro-Americans who would arrive centuries later, brimming with confidence at their power to conquer nature.

Tusayan is still there today, as a ruin, open to tourists. There is a small museum there, built partly by the Civilian Conservation Corps in the 1930s. Most of the CCC boys who worked on the museum came from Oklahoma and Texas, where a combination of drought and reckless farming practices had created the Dust Bowl and sent thousands of "Okies" packing their trucks and heading down Route 66 for California, just as the Ancestral Puebloans had fled their drought seven centuries before. Did the CCC boys look at the Tusayan ruin and see there a warning for their own times? Did they see the dangers of a society treating its land and other resources as if they were endless? Not really. American progress soon raced onward, to dam the Colorado River, fly to the moon, cure diseases, and build cities choking with cars and smog.

The collapse of Puebloan society happened in phases, with people retreating from one place to another, finally to a few enclaves—Hopi, Zuni, Acoma, and a string of pueblos along the Rio Grande River—where a farming way of life was still possible. The Puebloans could have continued living on their old homelands if they had been able to forget centuries of progress and revert to a hunting-gathering way of life, but human societies do not change easily. This left most of the Puebloan lands empty of humans. Nature does not like a void. Even as the Puebloans were retreating, several groups of hunter-gatherers were migrating toward the old Puebloan lands.

The same drought that brought down Puebloan society also made life very difficult for the hunter-gatherers who lived to the west, in the Mojave and Great Basin Deserts. Survival there had always been hard, and now it became impossible. People began migrating toward higher and cooler ground, the Colorado Plateau, which offered more rain, vegetation, and game. From the Mojave Desert came the Pai people (whom Americans would call the Hualapai), and from the Great Basin came the Southern Paiutes. They settled the western part of the Grand Canyon, the Hualapais on the south side and the Southern Paiutes on the north side.

In the lower deserts the Hualapais and Southern Paiutes had become masters of survival in the toughest of environments, and now on the Colorado Plateau their history and skills served them well. They lived in seasonal camps near water sources and traveled as the cycles of resources required. They hunted bighorn sheep and rabbits, gathered pine nuts, and roasted agave in rock-filled pits in the ground; today the Colorado River is lined with hundreds of roasting pits that grew steadily larger (sometimes twenty feet wide and seven feet tall) over generations of use. They wove brush into houses called wikiups and wove various plants into baskets so tight they could hold water. They watched Grand Canyon sunsets and pondered the mysteries of human life. The Hualapai place of creation is a mountain near the Colorado River, downstream from the Grand Canyon. For the Southern Paiutes, the souls of their dead enter the next world through the sinuous, waterfall-filled slot canyon of the Grand Canyon's Deer Creek.

At some water sources the Southern Paiutes did a limited amount of farming. On the other side of the river, in a major side canyon with rich soils, one band of Hualapai found a far more generous water supply, a reliable stream that flowed through a series of beautiful waterfalls and blue-green pools. This band of Hualapai became farmers and redefined themselves as a different people, the Havasupai, or "people of the blue-green waters." The Havasupai farmed in the warmer months, and in the winter they migrated to the plateau above to hunt and gather. They were reversing

FIGURE 2.3. Havasupai chief Watahomagie harvesting alfalfa in Havasu Canyon.

the seasonal pattern of the Ancestral Puebloans in the eastern Grand Canyon, who had spent summers on the rim and winters in the canyon, but for the Havasupai the rim was low and warm enough and their side canyon shady and wet enough that this pattern was manageable. The Havasupai roamed well east of their home canyon: they farmed at Indian Garden on today's Bright Angel Trail, and they added new pictographs to a rock-art panel (not far down the Bright Angel Trail from the rim) that already held Archaic and Ancestral Puebloan art. There are still abandoned Havasupai sweat lodges hidden in the woods not far from today's busy South Rim parking lots. Since the Havasupai are the only tribe that dwells within the Grand Canyon, the Hopis regard them as the guardians of the canyon.

As the Hualapais and Southern Paiutes were migrating toward the Grand Canyon from the west, the Navajos were migrating from the north. The Navajos had been migrating for a long time and a long way, all the way from a part of (today's) Alaska and British Columbia, where their Athabascan-speaking cousins still live. Even after many centuries of separation, Navajos can still hold a conversation with their northwestern cousins. When the Navajos found the recently emptied Ancestral Puebloan lands, they finally found a homeland for themselves. Indeed, they hit an environmental jackpot. Today the Navajos have the largest population and largest land base of any tribe in the United States.

The Navajos' new land was more generous than the lands found by the Hualapais and Southern Paiutes, and the Navajos made the most of it. As they migrated they encountered many landscapes and other tribes and cultures, and they readily borrowed ideas and mixed them with their own traditions; the most important thing they developed was a talent for adaptation. When the Spanish arrived with sheep, goats, and horses, the Navajos saw the possibilities and changed their whole way of life: grazing allowed a much broader harvesting of bioresources than did hunting and gathering. Sheep wool also made the Navajos world-famous weavers of rugs. A herd of sheep requires a large land area, so a grazing lifestyle left Navajo families thinly scattered on the land; even today, there are only a few Navajo towns with a population of a few thousand, and these were artificially stimulated by the presence of US government hospitals, schools, and other agencies. The Navajos lived in hogans, eight-sided homes made of timber and earth, which held a lot of spiritual symbolism, such as a door that faces east so Navajos can greet the rising sun. From the Puebloans, the Navajos learned how to grow corn in the desert. When Americans arrived, Navajos freely adapted ideas from them, too. Today as tourists travel from Desert View onto the Navajo Reservation, they see traditional hogans alongside solar panels and satellite dishes.

Of course, it has not been easy. After 1492 survival for Native Americans involved some very different challenges, ordeals, and abilities.

Only forty-eight years after Columbus landed in America, the Spanish conquistadores arrived in the Grand Canyon region. They were not seeking the Puebloans' knowledge about how to live humbly in a difficult environment. They were seeking conquest, gold, and empire. The Spanish had already rampaged through Mexico and brought down Aztec society. The Aztecs had possessed a lot of gold, and now the Spanish followed a legend that lands to the north held seven golden cities, Cibola. Instead, they found the Zuni and Hopi villages, made of humble stones. The Spanish conquered them anyway.

The Spanish extracted tribute and harsh servitude. For Puebloans who

tried to continue practicing their own religion, the Spanish inflicted tor-
ture and sometimes death. In 1680 the Pueblo peoples of Arizona and New
Mexico united and revolted against the Spanish and won temporary freedom, but the Spanish soon reconquered the New Mexico tribes. The Spanish never reconquered the Hopis, who were more physically isolated, leaving Hopi religious and cultural traditions more intact and alive than those
of most tribes.

Three centuries after the Spanish arrived in the Southwest, the growing
United States took possession of their old territories, and Americans began
settling the Grand Canyon region. Whereas the Spanish had ruled the
Southwest as a feudalistic empire, the United States was a far more open
and dynamic society, offering opportunities to poor Europeans. But from
the Native American viewpoint, this did not make any difference. Indeed,
American population growth brought much greater pressures on Native
lands.

Humans everywhere seem to be ethnocentric, ready to regard themselves as superior. Europeans and Americans had become so good at
inventing new technologies that Native Americans readily replaced their
pottery with steel buckets, their yucca sandals with boots, their bows and
arrows with rifles. But Euro-Americans took their technological superiority as proof of their superiority as a race and felt that Native Americans
were just another obstacle, like forests and buffalo, to sweep aside on their
way to their destiny.

As John Wesley Powell and his crew struggled down the Colorado River
in the summer of 1869, it is possible they were being watched by Navajos on
the rim of the Grand Canyon far above. Navajos had fled to the forests of
the South Rim to escape from Kit Carson, who a few years previously had
rounded up most Navajos and marched them hundreds of miles to cap-
tivity in New Mexico. Carson conducted a scorched-earth campaign, killing sheep, cutting down fruit trees, ruining wells, and burning crops and
hogans to make it impossible for Navajos to survive on their old lands. The
Grand Canyon became one of two major areas where the Navajos found
refuge, the other area being Navajo Mountain, near Glen Canyon; today
South Rim forests still hold the ruins of 1860s hogans. But it was hard to
hide from the rush of American history for very long.

Now American history was arriving inside the Grand Canyon, but awk-
wardly. John Wesley Powell and his men were running out of food and going

hungry. No Native American would be going hungry, for they would have recognized food all around them. The Americans were out of their natural habitat. Finally, Powell and his men came upon a garden full of squashes, stole some, and fled. It was a petty theft, and Powell was far more sympathetic to Native Americans than most of his contemporaries, but nevertheless it was symbolic that the first encounter of Americans and Natives inside the canyon was an act of theft by a people who did not understand this land.

The Hualapais had most of their lands taken away from them. Like the Navajos, they were subjected to a "Long Walk," back down into the unlivable desert they had fled many centuries before. The Santa Fe Railway wanted their few springs, cattlemen wanted their lands, and prospectors wanted to search for ores.

The Havasupai were stripped of all of their lands on the plateau above their canyon, which disrupted their seasonal migration pattern. When prospectors found ores near their village, the Havasupai reservation was contracted further to 518 acres around the village, and it did not include their famous waterfalls. Today one of those waterfalls is named Mooney Falls, but this is not a Native American tribute to the moon; it was named for a prospector, D. W. Mooney, who in 1882 was trying to rappel past the waterfall and fell to his death. When the Grand Canyon became a national park, the NPS sought to evict all private landowners and occupiers from within park boundaries, and they made no exception for the Havasupai farming at Indian Garden, who were evicted; at the same time the NPS was protecting Indian ruins like Mesa Verde, it was ruining life for living Native Americans. The NPS acquired the old mining claims in Havasu Canyon and incorporated them into the national park, against Havasupai protests, for this land included their waterfalls and cremation ground.

The Hopis and Zunis remained somewhat protected by their physical isolation, but their identities were assaulted. Their children were shipped off to government or church boarding schools; stripped of their pagan names, hairstyles, clothes, and religion; and forbidden to speak their own language. The Southern Paiutes lost access to most of their traditional lands and were confined to tiny, scattered reservations. In the name of assimilation, the federal government terminated their official status as a tribe in 1954. Yet Native Americans endured. After centuries of enduring droughts, social collapses, and migrations, they knew how to endure.

When the confinements of the Navajos and Hualapais went disastrously, they were released to return to their old homelands and rebuild their lives. The Havasupai worked for decades to regain title to their plateau lands, which were now part of the national forest system, and their waterfalls, which were now part of the national park. The Havasupai went to Washington, DC, and made a moral appeal and got their land restored in 1975. The Southern Paiutes got their tribal status restored in 1981. The Hopis and Zunis, supported by traditions that have endured for a thousand years, have withstood the culture shock of being absorbed into the United States, and now they find affluent but disillusioned Americans admiring their simple, spiritual way of life. The Navajos, with their talent for adaptation, are perhaps the most culturally dynamic tribe in the United States, their artists and musicians freely mixing Navajo traditions with the latest styles from American and world culture. In spite of their harsh treatment by the US military, many Navajos have served proudly in the military, and in World War II they turned their language into a secret military code in the Pacific—yet twenty years later Navajo children were still being whacked with a ruler for speaking their language in classrooms.

Today Native American culture is part of the cultural landscape of the Grand Canyon, and many visitors come seeking it. They find Navajo culture at the Cameron Trading Post, one of the few survivors of hundreds of trading posts that once dotted Navajo lands. Inside the park visitors find two tributes to Hopi culture: Hopi House and the Desert View Watchtower, the latter full of murals showing what the Grand Canyon means to the Hopis. At the ruins of Tusayan on the South Rim and Walhalla Glades on the North Rim, visitors find the stone footprints of the Ancestral Puebloans. The thousands of hikers who hike the eight-mile trail into Havasu Canyon meet the Havasupai in person. The Hualapais run their own rafting company on the Colorado River and built their glass-horseshoe Skywalk, which lures a million tourists per year away from Las Vegas casinos to encounter the canyon.

Tourism brought both opportunities and discomforts to Native Americans. They want the world to see and appreciate their story and culture, and tourism has allowed thousands of artisans to make at least a partial living from preserving their culture. Their arts embody their history: Navajo rugs embody centuries of sheep grazing, and Hopi pottery embodies a thousand years of storing seeds and carrying water. Yet Natives have also felt afflicted by tourists, who see them through a fog of stereotypes, expecting teepees and Great Plains headdresses, expecting savages or saints or exotic curiosities. The Santa Fe Railway and its corporate partner, the Fred Harvey Company, which took the lead at developing tourism in the Southwest and at the Grand Canyon, long pandered to these stereotypes, and even the Hopis who lived and worked at Hopi House seemed resigned to playing along: there is a famous photo of Albert Einstein standing in front of Hopi House in 1931, wearing a Sioux headdress. At the Cameron Trading Post and Monument Valley, the Navajos sell John Wayne souvenirs for Americans still enthralled with the saga of western conquest and Indian conquest. The Hopis in particular have been subjected to a kaleidoscope of American cultural projections: they were heathens, obstacles to Manifest Destiny, noble savages, picturesque images in paintings, classless utopians, victims of capitalism, peaceable sages, environmental paragons, and New Age seers. Even some academics have misunderstood and misused Hopi culture. These images and uses usually said more about American culture than about real Native Americans.

Surviving for two hundred years inside the Grand Canyon did require humans to be very real. Visitors looking into the Grand Canyon do tend to feel that Native American culture, with its immersion in the earth, fits this landscape. People see that even in nature's most enormous dimensions and eons and beauty, humans can belong.

CHAPTER THREE

Explorers
The Great Unknown

After thousands of years in which the Grand Canyon had been a well-trod home and a spiritual landscape for humans, another group of humans arrived on the North American continent, and for them the continent was so unknown that they imagined they were in India and defined the residents as "Indians." They defined the whole continent in contrast with European cities, technology, and agriculture, calling it "wilderness." In 1869 John Wesley Powell stood near an ancient ruin at the bottom of the Grand Canyon, a few miles from the spring the Hopis honored as their place of emergence, and he defined the canyon with what would become a famous phrase: "the great unknown."

Of course, for Powell the canyon was indeed unknown, dangerously unknown. Into the 1860s, after Americans had explored and mapped most of the West and founded thousands of towns there, the Grand Canyon and the surrounding region remained a large blank zone on the map. Americans knew this region held a great river and large canyons, but they knew few details. Some still hoped that the Colorado River would prove to be, like other great American rivers, a corridor for navigation, agriculture, mining, and settlement. Others imagined a river that disappeared into caverns, plunged over waterfalls, or disintegrated into monster whirlpools. Powell's journey was indeed an epic story of courage, skill, and endurance. The Grand Canyon became part of the larger story of Americans exploring and settling their continent, the story that would most define American national identity.

This story has usually been written from an English point of view, beginning with East Coast English colonies. Yet the Spanish were way ahead of the English at exploring and colonizing America. The Spanish reached the Grand Canyon in 1540, eighty years before the Pilgrims landed at Plymouth Rock. The Spanish exploration of the Southwest stretched from California to Kansas.

When the Coronado expedition reached the Hopi villages, the Hopis told them about a great river to the west. Great rivers were valuable to great empires. Coronado sent out a detachment of twenty-five men led by García López de Cárdenas, with some Hopi guides. The Hopis did not show the Spanish their salt pilgrimage trail into the canyon, but led them to the rim. Spanish accounts are too vague to be sure of exactly where they first saw the canyon, but it was probably in the stretch that holds today's Desert View, Lipan, and Moran overlooks.

Though the Spanish had already seen many canyons and mesas, they had never seen anything on the scale of the Grand Canyon, and they had trouble figuring it out. This still happens to tourists today. Cárdenas did correctly gauge the canyon to be about 10 miles across, but its depths tricked him. He estimated that the Colorado River was about 6 feet across—it is more like 300 feet. He imagined that it would not be difficult to reach the bottom. He and his men spent three days roaming along the rim, trying to find an easy route down, and when this failed they sent three of their most agile men to scramble down cliffs and around boulders. At the end of the day the men returned and reported that they had gotten only one-third of the way down. "What seemed to be easy from above," the official expedition report would say, "was not so, but instead very hard and difficult. . . . Those who stayed above had estimated that some huge rocks on the sides of the cliffs seemed to be about as tall as a man, but those who went down swore that when they reached these rocks they were bigger than the great tower of Seville."[1] This was Seville's cathedral tower, then 150 feet tall.

The Spanish were not trying to reach the river just because they were thirsty. They had already set in motion a plan to resupply the Coronado expedition by sending three ships, commanded by Hernando de Alarcón, up the Gulf of California and the Colorado River, which they were calling the "Firebrand River." When the Hopis told Coronado that a great river lay to the west, he correctly guessed that this was the same river Alarcón was trying to ascend. But Alarcón did not get far before the river's power stopped him. Hundreds of miles and hundreds of rapids separated Alarcón from Cárdenas. The Spanish decided that the Colorado River and its canyons were impassable and useless, and they left in disgust. No Europeans would return to the Grand Canyon for more than two centuries. The Spanish would devote their colonizing efforts to California, New Mexico, Texas, and southern Arizona and have very little presence in northern Arizona.

In 1776 a Franciscan padre, Francisco Tomás Garcés, wandered into the Grand Canyon alone, looking for souls to save. This was quite a contrast from the heavily armed conquistadores looking for gold. Garcés had much more respect for Native Americans. Guided by Natives along the way, Garcés followed the Colorado River from its mouth northward and onto the high plateaus of the western Grand Canyon, from which he looked down into the canyon, with its red river. It was Garcés who would give the river its enduring name, Rio Colorado, "river colored red" from its massive load of silt. He found his way into Havasu Canyon and was impressed by the Havasupai's irrigation system and fields full of crops. Garcés was still miles from the Colorado River, but it might be fair to call him the first white person to reach the bottom of the Grand Canyon. He saw the canyon with some of the nature-loving spirit of Saint Francis. For two centuries to come, the spirit of the conquistadores and the spirit of Saint Francis would contend over the Grand Canyon. Yet like most early white explorers, Garcés was seriously preoccupied by the "horror" of traversing the canyons: "I am astonished at the roughness of this country, and at the barrier which nature has fixed therein."[2]

Garcés left Havasu Canyon and followed the Grand Canyon's South Rim, heading for the Hopi villages. He "halted at the sight of the most profound caxone [*sic*] which ever onward continue; and within these flows the Rio Colorado."[3] The Havasupai had been very friendly to Garcés, but he found that the Hopis had come to fear the worst from whites. On July 4, 1776, they ordered him to leave. Five years later Garcés was caught in an uprising of tribes on the lower Colorado River and killed.

Garcés's journey also served a larger purpose. The Spanish wanted to find a route between Santa Fe, New Mexico, and Monterrey, California, and they knew that the Grand Canyon lay in between. Only a month after Garcés visited Havasu Canyon, two other Franciscan padres, Francisco Atanasio Domínguez and Silvestre Vélez de Escalante, along with a cartographer and eight other men, started off from Santa Fe to find a route that avoided the canyon by going well north of it. Such a route would also avoid the dry country and the increasingly unfriendly tribes on the canyon's south side. But in western Utah Domínguez and Escalante began running out of time and supplies, and they decided to head back to Santa Fe by crossing the Grand Canyon and picking up the now-known trail to the Hopi villages. Once again the Spanish were underestimating the canyon:

FIGURE 3.1. Father Francisco
Garcés descended into the
Grand Canyon in 1776.

the Paiutes warned them that crossing it was impossible. Heeding this
warning, Domínguez and Escalante headed east and followed the base of
the Vermilion Cliffs, which funneled them into the Echo Cliffs. Where the
cliffs met, the Colorado River emerged from Glen Canyon and began its

way into the Grand Canyon. This was the future site of Lees Ferry, the only river crossing for hundreds of miles. The padres sent their two strongest swimmers to try to cross the river, but they were nearly swept away. They built a crude raft, but again the river was too swift. Feeling trapped, they gave the place a name that translates as "let the errant brothers get out if they can." They did figure out an escape route to the north, and in Glen Canyon they found an easier place to cross the Colorado.

The tyranny of Spanish rule finally provoked Mexico to rebel and become independent in 1821, and this helped open the Southwest to Americans. The Spanish had prohibited Americans from exploiting their lands. In this era exploiting meant not gold prospecting, but fur trapping. Some Americans sneaked into northern Arizona anyway, for the Spanish had little enforcement there. Because beavers were found along rivers and the Colorado River was the great river of the Southwest, it is likely that some Americans found their way into the Grand Canyon. But they kept quiet about it, fearing Spanish retaliation. With Mexican rule, the restrictions were relaxed. In 1827 one group of trappers gave us the first account of Americans encountering the Grand Canyon.

James Ohio Pattie, in his early twenties, was a fur trapper from Kentucky who spent several years roaming the Southwest with his father and other trappers. The book he produced about his adventures is problematic for historians because it is full of typical mountain-man exaggerations and vagueness from Pattie not even knowing where he was. Historians cannot agree on whether Pattie traversed the Grand Canyon on the north side or the south side or where he managed to reach the river. But clearly Pattie was frustrated by how the canyon separated him from the river: "these horrid mountains, which cage it up, as to deprive all human beings of the ability to descend to its banks and make use of its waters."[4] When Pattie and his group got back to Santa Fe, the Mexican governor seized all their furs because they had not gotten a license.

In 1848 the United States, after its war with Mexico, took possession of the Grand Canyon and the rest of the Southwest and soon began sending expeditions to explore the region. In 1853 the Whipple expedition explored northern Arizona, not for the sake of science but to find the easiest route for the transcontinental railroad; the railroad needed to avoid canyons, so Whipple did not investigate the Grand Canyon.

In 1858 an American expedition finally reached the canyon, but this expedition too was motivated not by science but by nationalism. A decade previously, Brigham Young had turned Utah into a home for the Church of Jesus Christ of Latter-day Saints (the Mormons), and they had continued resisting federal authority. In 1857 the US Army sent a force to Utah to subdue the Mormons, yet the army's overland route was long, difficult, and plagued with supply problems. The army wondered if it would be easier to send men and supplies up the Colorado River, where they might get close to southern Utah, but no one was sure how far upstream the Colorado was navigable. To find out, Lieutenant Joseph C. Ives, who had served in the Whipple expedition, organized an expedition that was also authorized to explore what he called "Big Cañon."

Historian Earle Spamer has traced the earliest published use of the term *Grand Canyon* to a footnote in an 1857 climatological report by Philadelphia scientist Lorin Blodget. Blodget implied that this name was "known to trappers and hunters," so it may have been in circulation for years. The term *Grand Canyon* would be popularized by John Wesley Powell.[5]

Ives had a Philadelphia shipyard build a crude iron, open-decked steamboat, fifty-four feet long. The *Explorer* could not be too complicated, for it needed to be built in sections that could be disassembled and shipped west. At the mouth of the Colorado River the *Explorer* was reassembled, and at high tide on December 30, 1857, it was launched. The crew of a dozen men included John Strong Newberry, the first geologist to see the Grand Canyon.

The river was low, so the *Explorer* advanced slowly, and the crew had to get out and use ropes to drag it over sandbars. Native Americans watched them continually. Ives reported: "Their minds are active and intelligent but I have been surprised to find how little idea of the superiority of the whites they have derived from seeing the appliances of civilization. . . . In most respects they think us their inferiors. I had a large crowd about me one day, and exhibited several things that I supposed would interest them, among others a mariner's compass. They . . . thought we must be very stupid to be obliged to have recourse to artificial aid in order to find our way."[6] Likewise, Ives often viewed the Natives as inferiors. It was the collision of two worlds, of European technology and ancient American desert ways. A similar cultural collision occurred in Ives's perceptions of the land. He vacillated between seeing the land as "indescribably magnificent" and as appallingly desolate.

At the entrance to Black Canyon, which today holds Hoover Dam, Ives had a more serious collision: "We were shooting swiftly past the entrance, eagerly gazing into the mysterious depths beyond, when the Explorer, with a stunning crash, brought up abruptly and instantaneously against a sunken rock. . . . The concussion was so violent that the men near the bow were thrown overboard. . . . [T]he fireman, who was pitching a log into the fire, went half-way in with it; the boiler was thrown out of place; the steam pipe doubled up; the wheel-house torn away; and it was expected that the boat would fill and sink instantly."[7] The *Explorer* was repairable, but Ives had found the end of the navigable river. To try to reach the "Big Cañon" farther upstream, Ives led his men overland.

Guided by Hualapais, Ives reached the canyon rim near Diamond Creek. "The famous 'Big cañon' was before us; and for a long time we paused in wondering delight." As they descended to the river, "The sides of the tortuous cañon became loftier, and before long we were hemmed in by walls two thousand feet high . . . and the corresponding depth and gloom of the gaping chasms into which we were plunging, imparted an unearthly character to a way that might have resembled the portals of the infernal regions."[8] Reaching the river, which Ives had hoped to follow, he found it hemmed in by impassable cliffs.

Ives and his men returned to the rim and headed eastward. In one stretch the land offered no water for two days, and by the time they were heading into Havasu Canyon their mules, "with glassy eyes and protruding tongues, plodded slowly along, uttering the most melancholy cries." But their Havasu route proved impassable to mules, which had to be turned around and marched out. The men continued down the cliff-edge trail, which at one point held a "crazy looking" ladder made of sticks tied together with bark. When expedition topographer F. W. von Egloffstein tried the ladder, it broke and stranded him on the level below. He did go meet the Havasupai. To hoist Egloffstein back up, the men untied the leather straps from their muskets and knotted them together into a rope. They ended their exploration of Havasu Canyon, returned to the rim, and headed east, hundreds of miles, with more thirst and hardship along the way: "A more frightfully arid region probably does not exist upon the face of the earth."[9]

When Ives had been steaming up the river, with no worries about thirst, he had been inspired to write some poetic descriptions of the "majestic grandeur" of the canyons. But his overland ordeal left him more grudging.

After emerging from Havasu Canyon, he observed that "the rim country is cut into shreds by those gigantic chasms, and resembles a vast ruin." On the next page Ives wrote the most notorious lines ever written about the canyon: "The region last explored is, of course, altogether valueless. It can be approached only from the south, and after entering it there is nothing to do but to leave. Ours has been the first, and will doubtless be the last, party of whites to visit this profitless locality. It seems intended by nature that the Colorado river, along the greater portion of its lonely and majestic way, shall be forever unvisited and undisturbed."[10]

Today these lines are quoted by park rangers, river guides, and historians, who are smirking at Ives for being blind to the canyon's future as an international tourist destination. This was ironic, for Ives was the first white person to praise the canyon as "natural features whose strange sublimity is perhaps unparalleled in any part of the world."[11] Yet Ives was also typical of an era in which Americans were judging their land strictly for its economic value.

The Colorado River was never needed as a military route to Utah, for the trouble with the Mormons soon settled down. The Mormons thrived and began colonizing the region, founding hundreds of towns. They wanted to set up settlements in Arizona, but the Grand Canyon was a major obstacle. Jacob Hamblin, the Mormons' Daniel Boone, explored the possibilities for years, becoming the first white person to circumnavigate the canyon. Hamblin identified two places, just above and just below the canyon, that offered a reasonable route across the Colorado River and southward. The upper crossing was the same place that had defeated Domínguez and Escalante nearly a century before. The Mormons set up ferries at each site, Lees Ferry and Pearce Ferry. (A century later, these places would be the starting and ending points for Grand Canyon raft trips, though some trips leave the canyon at Diamond Creek, the access point used by Joseph C. Ives.) Lees Ferry was established in 1871 by John D. Lee, and its remoteness served him as a hiding place from justice; Lee had been a leader in the worst event of the Mormon troubles, the Mountain Meadows Massacre of 1857, in which Mormons had killed about 120 people from a wagon train passing through Utah. The law caught up with Lee in 1874 and executed him, but his ferry remained in operation until 1929, replaced by Navajo Bridge.

When the Powell expedition, seriously low on food, passed the future Lees Ferry in 1869, they saw only Native American ruins, and boatman Jack

Sumner commented, "It is desolate enough to suit a lovesick poet."[12] Three years later, when Powell returned on his second expedition, John D. Lee treated them to a feast of fresh fruits, vegetables, butter, and homemade beer. "The great unknown" quickly became American homelands. A dozen years later John Hance became the first American to settle on the canyon rim, and soon he was leading tourists down his trail to gawk at a rapid that had dismayed Powell.

When John Wesley Powell launched his river expedition at the town of Green River, Wyoming, on May 24, 1869, he was standing near the tracks of the transcontinental railroad, which had been completed with a golden spike at Promontory Summit, Utah, only two weeks previously. Powell had "shipped" his boats on the railroad from Chicago, and as he pivoted his boats into the river, they symbolized the pivoting between two eras. Until now, the American story had been a story of rivers, but now it would become a story of railroads.

When President Jefferson sent Lewis and Clark westward, they followed rivers, for rivers had always been the great transportation routes, the sinews of the nation. The great American cities were founded on rivers, the national economy ran on rivers, and the greatest engineering feat was a waterway, the Erie Canal. Rivers flowed through the American imagination, generating Mark Twain's steamboat iconography and Huckleberry Finn. John Wesley Powell literally gave his right arm for rivers: in the Civil War he was advancing up the Tennessee River with General Ulysses S. Grant when the Battle of Shiloh took his arm; later, he advanced down the Mississippi River and laid siege to Vicksburg.

Yet whereas Lewis and Clark and the western railroad surveys were generously funded by the federal government, Powell won only token support. American culture still celebrated heroic explorers, but only explorers who served national expansion, and Powell could not translate this into support for exploring an "altogether valueless" river locked inside canyons and choked with rapids. Powell had to cobble together his funding from other sources. As his crew took their first wobbly oar strokes down the river, the trains raced past, raced to build America's future, which would include delivering tourists to the Grand Canyon, to a rim memorial to John Wesley Powell and the exotic era of river explorers.

Before the Civil War Powell had rowed considerable distances on the Mississippi and Ohio Rivers, but he was unprepared for powerful

FIGURE 3.2. John Wesley Powell, December 1869, soon after he led the first river expedition through the Grand Canyon.

whitewater rivers. There were no experts to ask for advice. A few mountain men had blundered down sections of whitewater rivers, seeking transportation and profit, and gladly returned to solid land. Powell did something fundamentally new, choosing to run a major whitewater river for the adventure of it—if a scientific adventure—and this would make him a patron saint of future river runners.

Powell helped design wooden boats that had some good features for whitewater, such as watertight compartments that protected supplies and added buoyancy. But his designs were taken from boats used on lakes and harbors, with a keel that kept them heading straight ahead—a seriously bad idea for a whitewater river, where you need to maneuver through boulders. Powell avoided most of the big rapids by lining the boats alongshore or portaging them over the rocks, but the boats' heaviness made this a backbreaking task. Lifejackets were a new idea, and only Powell, unable to swim, wore one. The expedition became a race between self-education in whitewater and disaster.

Only two weeks into the trip, at a rapid Powell would name "Disaster Falls," disaster caught up with them. The crew of one boat failed to pull ashore atop the rapid and was swept into it. The boat smashed into rocks and was ruined; the crew barely escaped. One-third of the expedition's supplies were lost. They had come barely one-tenth their planned distance. The river was sure to get much worse. Instead of science, the trip was going to be about survival. The men were demoralized, and one of the men from the wrecked boat, Frank Goodman, quit at the first chance. The other two survivors, Oramel and Seneca Howland, after festering resentments with Powell, walked off the expedition near its end.

The bad feelings between Powell and the Howlands were probably planted before they ever met. Before he went down the Green and Colorado Rivers in 1869, Powell spent the summers of 1867 and 1868 exploring the Colorado Rockies with a group of friends, faculty, and students from Bloomington, Illinois. One of the civic leaders of Bloomington was Linus Graves, who had two distant cousins living in Colorado—Oramel and Seneca Howland. When Powell first arrived in Denver in 1867, it seems he was met by Oramel Howland, who occasionally worked as a printer for William Byers, the editor of the *Rocky Mountain News*. Byers was a relentless booster of Colorado and one of the last holdouts for the Colorado River being potentially navigable. Byers saw value in Powell's scientific survey of the Rockies, gave Powell a lot of publicity, and became Powell's leading financial backer. Byers joined Powell for the first ascent of Longs Peak in 1868, and it appears that for a while Byers was planning to go down the river with Powell.[13]

Half of the river crew came from Byers's circle: the Howland brothers, Byers's brother-in-law Jack Sumner, and two mountain men connected with Byers's trading post at Hot Sulphur Springs, Bill Dunn and Billy Hawkins. Now Powell was indebted to Oramel Howland for both his funding and his crew, but Powell was never good at acknowledging his debts. The other half of the crew was Powell, his brother Walter, and three men Powell happened across: George Bradley, Andy Hall, and Frank Goodman. At some point, Byers and Powell had a falling-out, and Byers cut off Powell financially. Powell was now stuck with Byers's friends, who had no idea how to row boats and no scientific abilities, and they were stuck with Powell, who could be tyrannical. The schism in the crew was infected by their troubles on the river. Powell blamed Oramel Howland for the wreck in Disaster Falls. Eventually, Howland instigated the walk off with his brother and Bill Dunn; the other two of Byers's men, Jack Sumner and Billy Hawkins, denounced Powell in later years.

From Disaster Falls the trip continued through a series of canyons, some named by Powell: Echo Park, Whirlpool, Split Mountain, Desolation, Gray, Labyrinth, Stillwater, Cataract, Glen. The heat turned their bacon rancid, and leakage turned their flour moldy, forcing them to throw away two hundred pounds; their only other food supplies were dried apples and coffee. Their efforts to fish and hunt usually failed. Their boats were spun in whirlpools, banged into rocks, swamped, and flipped, the men tossed overboard. The men were drenched by waves and storms, burned by the sun, blasted by sand. Their shoes and clothes were in shreds. They repeatedly had to search for pine sap to caulk leaking boats and driftwood to carve to replace lost and broken oars. Powell still tried to make scientific observations, and the men grumbled at the delay.

On August 5, two and a half months after the trip began, they started into the Grand Canyon. Powell had intended to take three times as long, but hunger and fear were forcing their pace. After 195 miles in mellow Glen Canyon, Powell now had "some feeling of anxiety" to see cliffs of harder rock rising downstream, for after observing the relationships between rock types and rapids, he recognized that "this bodes toil and danger."[14]

The toil and danger came soon and kept coming and got worse for 250 miles. The canyon got deeper and deeper. The crew seemed to be in a gloomy mood at the Little Colorado River, which George Bradley called "a lothesome [sic] little stream so filthy and muddy it fairly stinks."[15] Six years later Powell turned his sparse river journal into an eloquent book, *The Exploration of the Colorado River and Its Canyons,* and for their stop at the Little Colorado he wrote:

> Our boats, tied to a common stake, chafe each other as they are tossed by the fretful river. . . . We are three quarters of a mile in the depths of the earth, and the great river shrinks into insignificance as it dashes its angry waves against the walls and cliffs that rise to the world above; the waves are but puny ripples, and we but pigmies, running up and down the sands or lost among the boulders.
>
> We have an unknown distance yet to run, an unknown river to explore. What falls there are, we know not; what rocks beset the channel, we know not.[16]

Soon they came to Hance Rapid, a drop of thirty feet, the largest drop in the canyon, choked with rocks and holes—hydraulics where the water recirculates. Worse, at the bottom of the rapid the schist and granite emerged, the hardest rocks yet encountered, meaning harder rapids ahead.

Reinforcing the gloomy mood, the schist and granite formed a narrower, gloomy gorge with surrealistic rock fins and fangs. "We can see but a little way into the granite gorge," wrote Powell, "but it looks threatening."[17]

After lining Hance Rapid they arrived at a long chute of waves encased in sheer cliffs, impossible to evade. Powell and his crew had been running some rapids and improving their skills, but this rapid, Sockdolager, was to Jack Sumner "a perfect hell of waves" and to George Bradley "the worst one we have seen on the river.... [T]he waves were frightful ... and it seemed for a time that our chance to save the boats was very slim." They careened down the rapid, with Powell's boat swamped and, in his words, "unmanageable ... and we drift down another hundred yards through breakers—how, we scarcely know."[18]

The granite gorge continued for forty miles and included many of the canyon's worst rapids. The days were full of exhausting struggle, the boats were taking serious blows, and the mileage was frustratingly short. It took them twelve days to complete the one hundred river miles between Hance Rapid and Lava Falls, eight miles per day. Their baking soda got knocked into the river, so now their bread was unleavened, and they were down to their last sack of flour. Powell saw the canyon as "our granite prison."[19] Still, the men found time to marvel at the cliffs, the rain-induced waterfalls, and the abundant Indian ruins. At Lava Falls Powell was enthralled by its lava cascades, and he described them with the longest journal entry he made on the entire trip.

Sixty miles later, when the men were sure they had endured the worst and were near the canyon's end, they were in another granite gorge and ran into a rapid that seemed the worst yet, impossible to portage. They camped atop it and debated what to do. Oramel Howland decided to abandon the river and try to reach the Mormon villages to the north, and he persuaded his brother Seneca and Bill Dunn to join him. Even Powell wavered: "I almost conclude to leave the river. But for years I have been contemplating this trip. To leave the exploration unfinished, to say that there is a part of the canyon which I cannot explore, having already nearly accomplished it, is more than I am willing to acknowledge, and I determine to go on."[20] Powell and his remaining crew made it through Separation Rapid. Six miles later they met another nightmare, Lava Cliff Rapid, and barely survived it. This was the final danger.

The Howlands and Bill Dunn disappeared without a trace. In 1993 a

Utah historian claimed he had proof that the Howlands and Dunn had been killed by Mormons in the town of Toquerville, but a closer examination showed that his claims were fraudulent.[21] Most likely, the men were killed by the area tribe, but we may never know for sure.

In spite of all the hardships, Powell was determined to make another trip down the Green and Colorado Rivers, partly to make up for the lack of scientific results from the hurried first trip. He improved his boat design and selected a new crew that included several educators, though they remained amateurs as boatmen and scientists. Powell had met one, John F. Steward, an amateur geologist, when both were examining the fossils at Vicksburg. The second trip included a photographer, Jack Hillers, and an artist, seventeen-year-old Frederick Dellenbaugh, who would write a history of the expedition. This time Powell broke the river trip into segments, resupplied along the way, including at Lees Ferry. They headed into the Grand Canyon on August 17, 1872.

Once again, there were troubles and torments. The river was running much higher than in 1869. In one rapid Powell's boat capsized, and he was thrown into a whirlpool and sucked deep underwater. Dellenbaugh wrote, "We joked him a good deal about his zeal in going to examine the geology at the bottom of the river, but as a matter of fact he came near departing by that road to another world."[22] They struggled onward, and after three weeks in the canyon, halfway through, they arrived at Kanab Creek, where fresh supplies had been brought down. After resting two days, Powell quietly announced that this was the end of the river trip; they would hike out.

After Powell's expeditions, done for the sake of exploration, the river trips of the next half century—six of eight trips—were for finding and exploiting economic resources, culminating with a 1923 expedition searching for a site for what became Hoover Dam. After that, river trips were mostly for adventure.

If in the 1860s Americans had seen little value in the Colorado River, the gradual settlement of the Southwest would give the river a major value—as a water supply. When Americans first tried to settle the West, they applied the same strategies that had succeeded in the East and Midwest, where abundant rainfall and soil meant that a 160-acre farm could support a family. In exploring the arid Southwest, Powell saw clearly that old settlement habits were hopeless there. On his river trip Powell learned every day that nature was far more powerful than humans: if humans refused to obey the laws of water, they would die. With a river runner's eyes, Powell saw that American attempts to settle the West were violating the laws of water. Using his new stature as a leader of western exploration, Powell tried to warn the nation that national myths would need to yield to the laws of nature. Powell only aroused enormous hostility and ruined his career. He was swept aside by the high tide of Manifest Destiny, which had grown from a log-cabin folk belief into a juggernaut propelled by industrialism, Gilded Age capitalism, and the Wild West race for wealth.

CHAPTER FOUR

Exploiters

The Wild West Canyon

The three decades after John Wesley Powell's 1869 river expedition were the most expansive period in US history. The American population doubled, infused by millions of European immigrants seeking free farmland. Many immigrants never got beyond eastern cities, for the United States was becoming an industrial economy with millions of factory jobs. Industrialization created a huge demand for metals, including metals that had not been particularly valuable before. Copper had been used for kitchenware, but now copper's talent at conducting electricity made it essential for wiring, billions of miles of wiring. The need for metals stimulated a surge of prospecting and mining in the West. In the 1880s prospectors were finding massive copper deposits in southern Arizona, and prospectors began combing the rest of Arizona—including the Grand Canyon—looking for similar bonanzas. The arrival of railroads also made the West much more viable for ranching and logging, for now cattle and timber could be shipped to distant markets. To pursue these opportunities Americans flooded westward. Arizona's Euro-American population rose from 9,658 in 1870 to 122,931 in 1900. These decades would become mythic as the Wild West, a freewheeling scramble for wealth. Americans viewed themselves as the heroic conquerors of an abundant frontier, the land as a resource for exploitation. They made no exception for the Grand Canyon. The Wild West arrived at the canyon far ahead of America's conservation ethic.

The Wild West has left some powerful images in the American and world imagination: the whiskered prospector leading his burro through the desert and striking it rich, the covered wagon heading into a glorious horizon, the cowboy riding through a monumental landscape and shooting the outlaws or Indians who would deprive him of his earned rewards. In addition to cowboy heroism, Americans were embracing heroic technology, for this was the era of the railroad, the Brooklyn Bridge, and skyscrapers. By 1900 the Grand Canyon held hundreds of mining claims, the railroad was nearly there, rim lands were being grazed and logged and hunted, and engineers were dreaming of filling the canyon with hydroelectric dams.

By 1889 some men were making plans to build a railroad *inside* the Grand Canyon, down its entire length. Robert Stanton began dreaming of conquering the Grand Canyon when he was studying engineering in college, in 1869, and read about Powell's journey. Stanton misunderstood the canyon's width and imagined building a single-span railway bridge across it. This was only the first time Stanton would seriously underestimate the canyon, a tendency that later would prove deadly.

By 1889 Robert Stanton had earned a good reputation as an engineer and was the chief engineer of a new railroad company formed to build a railroad from Colorado to Southern California. In the Rocky Mountains the easiest routes for railroads were often river corridors, where rivers had carved openings and a steady grade through the mountains. The Southwest's greatest river was the Colorado River, and it ran between Colorado and Southern California, so Stanton and company president Frank Brown reasoned that their railroad should hug the Colorado River, right through the Grand Canyon. Their railroad would pay for itself by hauling coal from Colorado to booming Los Angeles, and it would open up new industries along the way. The Grand Canyon would be filled with mines, mining towns, and mills belching smoke. Stanton envisioned "each cove with its picturesque Swiss chalet, and its happy mountain people with their herds of sheep and mountain goats, developing business for our future railroad."[1] The railroad would run on electricity from dams on the Colorado River, and the wood for its bridges, ties, and tunnel timbers would come from the rim forests. The railroad would also be a popular ride for tourists. Above all, Stanton and Brown loved the idea of conquering the Grand Canyon.

On May 25, 1889, Stanton, Brown, and fourteen other men launched their boats onto the Green River in Utah to survey their railroad route. Their boats were grossly inappropriate for a whitewater river, with thin, brittle, leaky hulls and with rounded, narrow bottoms that let a boat roll over easily. John Wesley Powell had urged Stanton and Brown to take life jackets, but they did not bother. Powell had urged them to take experienced oarsmen, but two crewmen were rich lawyers who knew nothing about the laws of whitewater. Long before they reached the Grand Canyon, Stanton and Brown had lost two of their boats and most of their supplies.

A dozen miles into the Grand Canyon, Brown's boat flipped in a

FIGURE 4.1. Robert Brewster Stanton beside the Colorado River. He dreamed of building a railroad through the canyon and led the next river expedition after Powell.

whirlpool below Soap Creek Rapid, and he was sucked underwater and drowned. A dozen miles later the boat manned by Peter Hansbrough and Henry Richards flipped, and both men drowned. Richards was one of two African Americans on the crew.

Stanton decided to abandon the trip and escape up a side canyon.

Hoping to return, he cached his supplies in a cave in the canyon cliff, today called Stanton's Cave. Eight decades later archaeologists identified split-twig figurines in the cave as artifacts of the Archaic Culture, left as offerings of humility before nature's power. Perhaps Frank Brown had glimpsed such humility as he was drowning, but Robert Stanton remained convinced that Americans were more powerful than the Colorado River.

Six months later Stanton returned, leading another expedition. The day after they passed the spot where Frank Brown had drowned, their trip photographer, Franklin Nims, fell off a cliff and landed on rocks twenty feet below, but survived. After a long ordeal to evacuate the unconscious Nims by land, Stanton and his crew struggled downstream, wrecked boats, lost supplies, fell overboard, and nearly drowned; one man deserted. But they survived.

Stanton drew up plans for his railroad, which called for twenty miles of tunnels. He would blast off many cliffs to clear a passage and make rocky terraces to support tracks, and he would build numerous bridges across side canyons. In his river diary Stanton occasionally admitted that the canyon was beautiful, but he noted that the Redwall Limestone "would not be so when quarried."[2] Stanton campaigned to find investors, but he could not persuade them that his plans made financial sense. Later, Stanton caught another Colorado River dream and built a boat to dredge for gold in Glen Canyon. Another illusion.

In promoting his railroad, Stanton made highly overoptimistic claims about the mineral wealth inside the Grand Canyon, and this helped attract more prospectors. They found the canyon tempting, for the Colorado River had already done their digging for them, exposing massive faces of rocks.

Stanton's river trip probably encouraged four small, do-it-yourself Grand Canyon river trips between 1896 and 1908, led by George Flavell, Nathaniel Galloway, Elias Benjamin "Hum" Woolley, and Charles Russell. Typical of the opportunists of the Wild West, they had managed to make a living through prospecting, hunting, and trapping but always kept an eye out for a bigger chance—they would not find it in the canyon.

Far more prospectors arrived by foot, but most took one look from the rim and turned around and left for easier landscapes. Locating ore inside the canyon, building a trail to it, and hauling out ore would require extraordinary effort. It would take eccentric, tough, determined, larger-than-life characters to match the canyon. Perhaps they liked the heroic challenge of

FIGURE 4.2. John Hance, prospector and storyteller, the first American pioneer to settle at the canyon, on the Bright Angel Trail.

prospecting there, but a few also fell under the canyon's spell and loved the idea of calling it home.

The Wild West image of the lone prospector who strikes it rich did sometimes really happen: the silver strike in Tombstone, Arizona, worth thirty million dollars, was made by one eccentric prospector. Of course, Wild West iconography was seldom the whole story. Mining in Arizona was soon dominated by Gilded Age corporations. Yet at the Grand Canyon the Wild West iconography held true. Most prospecting was done by rugged, eccentric individuals, some with long white beards and with a burro or two. Sometimes a few prospectors teamed up, especially when they needed to turn a claim into a mine.

There were probably hundreds of prospectors who wandered into the canyon, and almost all left miserable, defeated, unremembered. The canyon's sedimentary rocks might be rich in beauty, but they held almost no gold or silver. They did hold copper and also asbestos, important for fireproofing in an age when most cities were made of wood and most indoor lighting was made of flame. But the canyon's copper and asbestos deposits were usually limited in extent, and only a half dozen of them justified building a trail, digging a mine, and hauling ore out of the canyon on mules or burros. When the ore got to the canyon rim, the railroad was still sixty miles away, and the nearest available copper smelter was in El Paso, Texas. All these expenses meant that even high-grade ore was barely profitable.

The first white person to settle permanently on the canyon rim was John Hance, in 1883. Born in the Tennessee mountains, John Hance grew up in the Missouri Ozarks amid limestone cliffs and a major lead-mining area. Hance absorbed a lot of prospecting lore, and when the Pikes Peak gold rush broke out in 1859 he caught the fever and headed for Colorado, but had no luck. In the Civil War Hance served in the Confederate army and served time in a Union prison, and after the war he went to work driving wagons for the US Army out of Fort Leavenworth in Kansas, a job that eventually led him to Arizona. When prospecting fever broke out in Arizona, Hance caught it anew and took on the Grand Canyon.

On a ledge about eight hundred feet above the Colorado River, Hance found a rich vein of asbestos. If it had been located elsewhere, it would have made Hance rich. But it was located on the north side of the Colorado River, and Hance had to haul the ore in a little wood and canvas boat that wobbled across the tailwaters of one of the most ferocious rapids in the Grand Canyon, today called Hance Rapid. Hance built a steep trail, soon wiped out by a landslide, and then a new trail along a different route. Some Grand Canyon asbestos made it all the way to Europe, where it was sewn into the stage curtains of famous theaters full of glamorous people. Yet John Hance remained in patched clothes, cooking beans on a lonely campfire.

The first white woman to settle at the canyon was Ada Diefendorf Bass, in 1895. Ada was a twenty-six-year-old music teacher who had studied at a prestigious music conservatory in Boston. From New York State, Ada traveled to Arizona to visit an aunt. Ada wanted to see the Grand Canyon and went there with prospector and tour guide William Wallace Bass.

William Bass had been a railroad dispatcher in New York City when he suffered a nervous breakdown, and his doctor recommended a change of climate and lifestyle. Bass came to Williams, Arizona, in 1883, first living in a cave. He went to the Grand Canyon, hoping to strike it rich, and he located some good deposits of copper and asbestos and continued working them for years. But Bass soon developed a deeper enthrallment with the canyon. Like John Hance, Bass decided that tourists too would be enthralled. He built a South Rim tourist camp, a trail into the canyon, and roads from the railroad and started a stagecoach to bring tourists to his camp. One day, along came Ada.

Bass was a charmer who played the violin, wrote poetry, told amazing stories, and studied astronomy books at his prospecting camps. Ada was charmed by the canyon and by the man who had mastered it; they married.

It was not easy. Ada endured thirty years of isolation, poverty, and very hard work. There was little water at their rim home, so when it was time to do the laundry Ada packed it onto a burro and took it seven miles down the trail to the Colorado River and then back out. Sometimes when they had money to spare, William went into town and drank it away. Sometimes he went prospecting in the canyon for months and left Ada on her own. When Ada first became pregnant, she went home to New York and did not return for three years. She had four children, the first white family raised at the canyon. As their tourist business grew, Ada had to cook and clean for guests, too. At least their house had a piano.

William Bass built a cable car to cross the Colorado River, an inner-canyon camp with orchards and vegetable gardens, and a trail to the North Rim. As with Hance's trail and almost all the other trails that would be built

FIGURE 4.3. William Wallace Bass, prospector and tourist guide, with his burro Joe and his dog Shep, on the canyon rim, ca. 1899.

into the canyon, Bass followed routes originally tramped by bighorn sheep, deer, and other animals looking for food or water and then used by the Native Americans who hunted and farmed in the canyon. Yet Native Americans had not used pack animals, so Bass had to make major improvements to allow passage for burros, mules, or horses. In a cave Bass built a photography lab and developed his canyon photos, which he showed on long tours of eastern cities. William and Ada were united by their love of the canyon, but even in death they were not in sync. William had his ashes scattered over Holy Grail Temple, whereas Ada was buried in the South Rim's Pioneer Cemetery.

Louis Boucher was born in Quebec, Canada, and showed up at the Grand Canyon by 1891. He found deposits of copper and graphite near the Colorado River and built a trail (today's Boucher Trail), which he called the Silver Bell Trail for the bell worn by his favorite mule. About fifteen hundred feet below the rim, he built a tent camp at Dripping Spring, where water drips from a large, shady overhanging cliff. Near his claim at the canyon bottom, he built a rock cabin and planted a vegetable garden and an orchard with seventy-five fruit trees. Boucher needed the food, for his mining did not earn much profit.

One of the few Grand Canyon prospectors who did find a rich lode was Pete Berry. Berry had been a miner in Colorado and came to Flagstaff to run the saloon of his brother John, who was killed while trying to break up a barroom brawl; John's friends broke into the Flagstaff jail and shot one killer and lynched the other. Pete married his brother's widow, but she got tired of Pete—or got tired of his long absences while prospecting in the canyon—and ran off with a traveling salesman.

On Horseshoe Mesa beneath Grandview Point, Berry and his partners located a copper lode that would produce $75,000 of ore. They sent one seven-hundred-pound block of ore to the 1893 Columbian Exposition in Chicago, and it won an award for being 70 percent copper (most of the mine's ore was only half that pure). Berry spent $12,000 to build and maintain a trail to the mine, today's Grandview Trail, and it also cost a lot of money to maintain mule teams. By 1902 Berry had decided that the mine was not worth all its trouble, and he sold it for $1,875; the buyer soon turned around and sold the mine to a speculator for $40,000. A few years later the price of copper fell steeply, and the mine closed. Berry used his mining profits to build a new hotel at Grandview, alongside the rustic Grandview Hotel he had opened in 1897. In 1913 Berry sold his Grandview lands to newspaper baron William Randolph Hearst, who for the next three decades would fight off the attempts of the NPS to add these lands to the park.

Seth Tanner explored the eastern section of the canyon beneath Desert View, found some minor copper deposits scattered along the river, and helped build today's Tanner Trail. The Tanner Trail later became known as the Horse Thief Trail when rustlers used it to drive stolen horses across the canyon, connecting with the Nankoweap Trail to get to the North Rim. The thieves sold Arizona horses in Utah and then stole Utah horses, rebranded them, and drove them across the canyon to sell them in Arizona. In the 1920s, during Prohibition, bootleggers set up a still on the Tanner Trail to make liquor to sell in Grand Canyon Village.

William O'Neill got his nickname, "Buckey," from a gambling term, *bucking the tiger,* for someone who stakes everything on one bet. Buckey O'Neill's brashness made him a Wild West legend and made a big difference in Grand Canyon history—and it also got him killed.

O'Neill arrived in Arizona in 1879, just in time to live in Tombstone and gamble and drink alongside Wyatt Earp and Doc Holliday. Born in St. Louis, the son of an Irish immigrant who fought in the Irish Brigade in the Civil War, O'Neill quoted Horace Greeley to explain why he was going west, to the land of opportunity for a young man. O'Neill worked as a typesetter and reporter in Tombstone and Prescott and then got elected Yavapai County sheriff. He became famous for catching outlaws, especially a gang who robbed the Atlantic and Pacific Railroad, which was building the first tracks across northern Arizona. Yet O'Neill considered the Atlantic and Pacific Railroad itself to be a robber for not paying fair tax rates, and he promised voters to make them pay up. He twice ran for territorial delegate to the US Congress as a Populist, opposing railroad and other monopolies, but he lost.

Though Tombstone and Prescott were booming mining towns, O'Neill was not infected by prospecting fever until the Grand Canyon added its charisma to the fever. O'Neill did some prospecting inside the canyon, but it was twenty miles south of the canyon that he found copper in the limestone ground, which became the Anita Mine in 1897. Although other prospectors had been defeated by the Grand Canyon's distance from a railroad, O'Neill decided to build a railroad. For financial backing he went to the Santa Fe Railway, which was absorbing the Atlantic and Pacific Railroad, but the Santa Fe declined; it probably did not help that O'Neill had been so antirailroad. O'Neill went to eastern and local investors and raised enough money to start building a spur line from Williams to Anita and the canyon. O'Neill recognized the canyon's potential for both mining and tourism. But the railroad barely made it to Anita before it failed, for the copper veins there proved superficial. O'Neill sold out his investment, and a few years later the Santa Fe Railway completed his railroad to the canyon. O'Neill would not live to see it. With the outbreak of the Spanish-American War, O'Neill signed up to be a commander of Teddy Roosevelt's Rough Riders in Cuba. O'Neill admired Roosevelt's progressive political views, and Roosevelt loved O'Neill's genuine Wild West persona. During the charge up the San Juan Heights, O'Neill, who had sometimes declared that "the Spanish bullet isn't molded that can kill me," ignored a warning that he keep his head down, and he was promptly shot in the head and killed.[3]

The same battle made Teddy Roosevelt a national hero and helped make him president. Roosevelt shared a lot of O'Neill's brashness; it was both personal brashness and national brashness. Yet Roosevelt had decided that

America's pioneer brashness about conquering nature was a problem that needed to be attacked.

Another of Roosevelt's Rough Riders, Dan Hogan, came home alive and went back to work on the copper lode he had found in the Grand Canyon a decade before. To reach his Orphan Mine, Hogan built a "trail" of ropes, ladders, and stone toeholds down the sheer cliffs near today's Maricopa Point. Hogan worked his mine only occasionally, as it required shoveling aside tons of worthless dark rock to extract the copper. Finally, he gave up mining, and in 1936 he opened a small tourist lodge and saloon on his claim on the rim. In 1946 Hogan sold his land and business for fifty-five thousand dollars; a few years later, geologists discovered that the worthless dark rocks Hogan had been dumping into the canyon were some of the richest uranium ores in America, worth many millions of dollars. Until 1969 uranium was mined right in the middle of a busy national park. Uranium ore was dumped into open-bed trucks, and uranium dust floated over the tourists lounging around the adjacent motel swimming pool. The ore was hauled through the park roads; one local child recalled picking up a fallen piece of ore and taking it home as a novelty. Some of the miners and truck drivers died of cancer, but Dan Hogan lived to be ninety years old.

The uranium mine remained in operation inside the park because 1870s mining laws granted landownership that was legally unassailable. These laws were intended to reward prospectors for taking the risks of pioneering. All a prospector needed to do was to file a claim, prove that the claim held legitimate ore deposits, and do some work on the claim, and then even the federal government that had granted ownership had no means for revoking it. Even when President Teddy Roosevelt designated the Grand Canyon a national monument in 1908, he had no authority to overturn established mining claims. Although the era of copper mining in the canyon was fairly brief and unprofitable, it would cast a long shadow into the future, dimming hopes for turning the canyon into a national park. Two of Arizona's first three US senators, Henry Ashurst and Ralph Cameron, had Grand Canyon prospecting in their blood, and they would remain more loyal to pioneer land rights than to the concept of national parks. Most Arizonans felt the same way. If the Grand Canyon had possessed more mineral wealth, this opposition would have made more sense economically, but it was mainly fueled by cultural values, by the national belief that the land was meant to be exploited.

One of the first prospectors to locate copper deposits in the canyon was William Henry Ashurst, the father of the future senator. Ashurst made most of his living from ranching near Flagstaff, but in the winters he roamed the canyon looking for ores, sometimes with John Hance. In 1901, after twenty years of prospecting, Ashurst was alone in the canyon when a random rock slide caught him and pinned him to the ground. He died a long, lonely death. John Hance found his body many weeks later. Ashurst's son Henry inherited his father's outgoing personality, and it helped get him elected to the US Senate when Arizona became a state in 1912. Henry Ashurst sympathized with all the Arizonans who opposed making the Grand Canyon a national park, yet he saw that the canyon's popularity with tourists probably made a park inevitable, so he wrote a bill that established a park but protected private land rights and left out most of the forests on the rim. For Henry Ashurst, private land claims were not just an abstract ideal but something his father had died for.

At least Henry Ashurst cooperated to make the Grand Canyon a national park. His fellow senator Ralph Cameron did his best to sabotage the park, even after it was established. In 1883 Ralph Cameron was twenty years old and working in a Boston department store when he read about John Wesley Powell's Grand Canyon adventures. Cameron was enthralled and headed west. He settled in Flagstaff and worked at various jobs and businesses, and in his free time he and his friends and his brother Niles roamed inside the canyon, searching for ores. In 1890 Ralph Cameron helped Pete Berry find and claim the rich copper deposits beneath Grandview Point. As Cameron observed the challenges and failures of canyon mining, he also noticed that tourism was rising fast.

Both Ralph Cameron and Pete Berry went into the tourism business, but Cameron was much shrewder about it than Berry. Berry remained at Grandview, which would be left stranded by the arrival of the Santa Fe Railway a dozen miles to the west. Cameron recognized where the railroad was likely to arrive, and he planned ahead. He filed hundreds of mining claims totaling thousands of acres on the canyon rim, along the Colorado River, and along the Bright Angel Trail, which Cameron and Berry had helped build in 1891. These mining claims were mostly bogus, holding no valuable ores, but mining laws gave Cameron a strong legal grip on the land. His grip was strengthened by his flourishing political career. In 1891 he became the first sheriff of Coconino County, which included the Grand Canyon, and in

1905 he was elected county supervisor. Cameron built a hotel on the rim and a camp at Indian Garden on the Bright Angel Trail, and he made major improvements to the trail. He turned the Bright Angel Trail into a toll road, charging one dollar per person (about twenty dollars in today's money); it would become the only toll road in any national park. When Cameron's legal right to charge a toll expired and the rights reverted to Coconino County, Cameron arranged for the county to lease the trail back to him.

When the Santa Fe Railway arrived, it did bring Cameron a lot of business, but it was also a powerful rival and challenged Cameron's land claims and tolls. The Santa Fe formed a partnership with the Bright Angel Hotel, next to Cameron's Hotel, and it forbade Cameron's agents from soliciting customers at its train station. The rivalry became nasty, with agents of both sides carrying guns. Cameron felt himself to be an authentic pioneer hero who had played by the code of the frontier, taking risks and working hard to earn his rewards, but now he had to compete against a giant corporation. This was the end of the Gilded Age, in which railroads were despised robber barons, and Cameron, a genius at public relations, portrayed himself as a common-man pioneer resisting tyranny. This image got Cameron elected as territorial delegate to the US Congress in 1908 and to the US Senate in 1920.

The Santa Fe Railway wanted its customers to have access to the canyon, so it challenged Cameron's control of the Bright Angel Trail. When this challenge failed, the Santa Fe was forced to build its own trail, the Hermit Trail. It also built an eight-mile rim road—Hermit Road—to the trailhead and a tourist facility inside the canyon, Hermit Camp. Ralph Cameron used his land claims on the West Rim to try to stop the Santa Fe from building its road and trail. Years later, the NPS tried to get control of the Bright Angel Trail, and it too failed and was forced to build its own trail, the South Kaibab. Cameron would not even allow the NPS to build an outhouse or clean up the junk at Indian Garden.

Cameron could be petty, but he was dreaming big. He wanted to build his own 14-mile scenic railway along the canyon rim and a cable railway into the canyon. He pushed a series of schemes to build a hydroelectric dam on his claims at the base of the Bright Angel Trail. One dam would be 230 feet high and create a reservoir 15 miles long, its power used primarily for mining operations throughout Arizona. Other schemes would harness the stream dropping from Indian Garden to the river and build at Indian Garden a mill to extract (nonexistent) gold from Colorado River sands.

Cameron also planned to pump water from Indian Garden to a great ranch he would build on the rim. Cameron bragged that he intended to "make more money out of the Grand Canyon than any other man." He did not care whether his profits came from showing off the canyon or marring it. The canyon was the American frontier, and the frontier existed to make pioneers rich. Ralph Cameron would become a powerful opponent of Grand Canyon National Park. Future NPS director Stephen Mather would regard Cameron as the NPS's worst enemy.

The Wild West era also saw a boom in ranching in the Grand Canyon region. In 1873 Arizona had only 40,000 cattle; by 1891 it had about 1.5 million, many brought in by Texans. Yet Arizona was quite different from Texas: it was much drier, its topsoil was poorer, and the grasses were less resilient. When Arizona ranchers packed as many cattle onto an acre as on Texas ranches, the cattle soon exhausted the grasslands, and the soil began eroding. In the 1890s hundreds of thousands of cows died of starvation and thirst, and thousands of ranches were doomed to eventual failure. In 2010 Arizona supported about 900,000 cattle, and Texas supported fourteen times as many, though it is only 2.3 times as large as Arizona.

Cattle grazing even reached inside the Grand Canyon by the 1880s. In its western sections the canyon widens out and creates a broad platform—the Esplanade—a thousand feet or more below the rim. North Rim ranchers built a half-dozen trails onto the Esplanade and drove their cattle there for the winter and then back up onto the Kaibab Plateau in the spring. Yet Kaibab Plateau meadows were alpine meadows, too fragile for heavy grazing. On the South Rim cattle grazing stretched right up to the rim. Both rims also held sheep grazing, also a poor fit for the ecosystem.

On the North Rim the ranching was operated by the United Order of Orderville, Utah. Mormon leader Brigham Young created the United Order in the 1870s to encourage cooperative economics throughout Utah; it helped inspire Edward Bellamy's Christian socialist utopian novel *Looking Backwards* (1888). In Orderville the United Order reached its most extreme form, outright communism that abolished private property and shared everything equally, including meals in a communal dining room. In an era when the rapidly industrializing Western world was debating the problems and merits of capitalism and socialism, the Grand Canyon offered a unique laboratory, with the South Rim being run by capitalists and the North Rim by theocratic communists. Which side did better at managing their lands?

Neither. The communists overexploited their ecosystem just as badly as the capitalists.

The forests of northern Arizona looked like gold to the Santa Fe Railway, whose main line from Chicago to Los Angeles ran mainly through prairies and deserts and pinyon-juniper forests, which makes poor lumber. Northern Arizona holds the world's largest forest of ponderosa pines, tall and thick and good for lumber. The railroad needed a lot of lumber for ties, bridges, earthworks, and stations and for exporting to all the booming towns and cities along its route. Their tracks ran right through the forests around Flagstaff and Williams, so there was no urgency about logging the ponderosa forests on the rim of the Grand Canyon fifty miles away, but the possibility of doing so was a rationale for logging companies to oppose the creation of a national park and later for drawing the park's boundaries very close to the rim. By the 1920s the forests around Flagstaff and Williams had been logged heavily. Lumber mills were designed to take sixteen-foot sections of a tree, and often the lumberjacks took only the fattest sixteen feet and left most of a tree to rot. Logging finally moved north to the canyon. As with ranching, logging in northern Arizona was done by people from other states and climates, places where trees grow much faster, where clear-cut forests soon rebound by themselves. Arizona pioneers did not understand that those big ponderosa trees were four hundred years old and that if they clear-cut the forests they were cutting off the future of logging. The Michigan timber company that set up operations just outside the boundary of Grand Canyon National Park, with tracks and two dozen spurs that ran for many miles along the boundary, cut the forests as if they were Michigan forests. The regrowing forests were grossly overgrown with baby trees, and policies of fire suppression allowed debris to accumulate on the forest floor for decades, guaranteeing a future of massive unnatural wildfires.

The Wild West era also included a free-for-all of hunting, as if wildlife were inexhaustible and ecological laws did not exist. In the forests of the North Rim, mountain lion hunts became a popular sport, encouraged by novelist Zane Grey's writings about his hunting adventures there. One tied-up mountain lion was brought across the canyon on a horse and kept caged outside El Tovar Hotel for the amusement of tourists. When the Grand Canyon Game Preserve was established on the North Rim in 1906 for the sake of deer (and deer hunters outside the preserve), Jimmy Owens was hired as game warden—to eliminate the predators that preyed on deer. He killed more than five hundred mountain lions, plus a lot of bobcats, coyotes, and wolves. The deer population began rising dramatically and severely overgrazed the forests and grasslands. Too late, forest managers realized they had created a big problem. In 1924 a Flagstaff rancher named George McCormick proposed a solution: he would round up thousands of deer, drive them down the Nankoweap Trail to the Colorado River, swim them across, and drive them up the Tanner Trail to South Rim forests. McCormick seemed to think deer could be herded just like cows. It was more like herding cats. The deer drive became big news; Zane Grey came to write about it, and filmmaker D. W. Griffith came to film it. McCormick organized more than one hundred men into a line; they marched and rode through the forest, yelling and ringing bells to scare the deer toward the trailhead. The deer inside this human corral were indeed scared, but they turned and ran through the gaps between the herders and disappeared into the forest. By the time the herders converged near the trailhead, all the deer had escaped.

The deer did not escape their fate the next two winters, when many thousands of deer starved to death. For decades to come, college biology textbooks included the case study of the North Rim deer, whose population rose from about four thousand in 1906 to as many as one hundred thousand in 1924 and then quickly crashed by tens of thousands. Today's wildlife experts believe these figures were exaggerated, but there was no question that the pioneers once again had failed to understand the southwestern environment. Even Zane Grey, who usually championed pioneer values, criticized antipredator policies.

Very quietly, the canyon's Wild West era began to dissipate and yield to something else. The end started as quietly as the steps of a few horses emerging from the forest at John Hance's cabin, ridden by people who wanted to see the Grand Canyon. They were happy to pay Hance for water and a cooked meal and a place to camp and for his taking them into the canyon on his trail. The era of Grand Canyon tourism had arrived.

By 1886 John Hance was advertising his services as a tourist guide. Soon he was making more money from tourists than from mining. Around the campfire he told tall tales. He told about the time his horse began falling into the canyon with Hance still on him. Hance waited patiently until his horse was only a few feet from hitting the ground and yelled, "Whoa!" His horse was so well trained that he stopped in midair, and Hance stepped off. Tall tales were a long American tradition, generated by pioneers encountering the forces of nature, and now Hance was stretching this tradition further to make it fit the Grand Canyon. He became a famous storyteller, and eventually the Santa Fe Railway hired him just to tell canyon tales.

Other prospectors too saw the tourists arriving, and they did not need much persuasion to switch from mining to tourism. William Bass, Louis Boucher, Pete Berry, and Ralph Cameron turned their trails into tourist trails and built lodging on the rim or inside the canyon. Most of them would be left stranded in the wrong places and be put out of business when the Santa Fe Railway arrived. Pete Berry's rustic hotels at Grandview, reachable from Flagstaff by a stagecoach that cost twenty dollars and required a long day on horrible roads, could not compete with the Santa Fe's luxurious El Tovar Hotel, reachable by a comfortable four-dollar train ride.

Most of the Grand Canyon's pioneer prospectors finally drifted away in defeat and bitterness. They had made heroic efforts to find metals to serve the United States, but now the industrial America they had helped build, in the form of Santa Fe Railway locomotives, arrived at the canyon and ran them over. It was their copper that lit the electric lights of El Tovar Hotel, rendering their own hotels archaic. They had played by the rules of American pioneering; they were rugged individuals who had taken risks and suffered hardships, and they felt they deserved to be rewarded.

Yet in the decades between 1869 and 1900, the rules of American society had changed quite a bit. It was the Gilded Age, in which economic power was increasingly concentrated in the hands of giant corporations and robber barons. Millions of ordinary farmers and factory workers felt that their American Dream was being run over by a train. Gradually, a counterbalancing effort took shape, the Progressive movement, and abruptly in 1901 it took over the White House—Teddy Roosevelt became president. Roosevelt also brought into power another movement that had been slowly gathering strength, the conservation movement. Roosevelt's presidency began a lasting change in the way Americans perceived the Grand Canyon and the rest of nature. Natural resources would become natural wonders. The Wild West would become the western wilderness. Arizona would go from being the "Copper State" to being the "Grand Canyon State." Yet America's frontier values remained very powerful, and they would not yield easily.

CHAPTER FIVE

Conservation
"Leave It as It Is"

Four days in September 1901 were the most pivotal days in Grand Canyon history.

On September 17, 1901, the first scheduled Santa Fe Railway train arrived at the South Rim. The railroad would bring millions of people to the canyon and let them have a powerful experience of it.

Santa Fe Railway executives should have thrown a big celebration for the first train's arrival, but the day turned out to be very somber. The previous day a train had brought the casket of President William McKinley to Washington, DC, and today the assassinated president was lying in state in the Capitol. America's railroad executives were probably more somber today than most Americans, for McKinley had been replaced in the White House by Teddy Roosevelt, an enemy of railroads and other monopolies, a crazy fool who loved trees and rocks more than he loved national prosperity. As McKinley had lain dying, no one had been able to find Roosevelt, for he had been off with his family climbing a mountain in the Adirondacks, just for the fun of it.

Roosevelt became president on September 14, three days before the Santa Fe's first train arrived at the canyon. Both events were necessary for the canyon to become a national park. The canyon needed a lot of visitors, and it needed someone to convince those visitors why they should care about protecting it. It needed both tourists and conservation values. Tourism and conservation would not always fit together smoothly. But the Grand Canyon would create common ground even for railroad barons and Teddy Roosevelt.

Yet first the Grand Canyon and other natural wonders helped unite the contradictory forces inside Teddy Roosevelt himself. His personal story is worth a moment of study, for it embodied and led the change of eras and values that America itself underwent.

Born in 1858, Teddy grew up in the glory days of the Wild West, and he

FIGURE 5.1. The first Santa Fe Railway passenger train to arrive at the canyon, September 17, 1901. It would take another eighteen years for the canyon to become a national park.

loved the frontier mystique and made great efforts to embody it. Roosevelt also grew up bird-watching and collecting animal bones, loving nature for its own sake. The frontier he loved was that of brave, solitary frontiersmen like Daniel Boone, but now America's ethos of frontier conquest was armed not with a long rifle but with the machinery of an industrial nation, and it was threatening to overwhelm America's nature. The average American might not see or worry much about the conflict between America's frontier values and its natural wonders, but for Teddy Roosevelt, with his huge enthusiasm for both, this contradiction was a big problem. He took it more personally and was forced to wrestle with it. Psychologist Erik Erikson, who coined the phrase *identity crisis*, has studied how powerful historical forces can intersect within one individual, create an intense conflict, and generate a solution, a solution that the individual can then offer to a people to solve their historical impasse. Teddy Roosevelt never gave up loving America's frontier mystique, but he did decide that it could not be allowed to ruin America's nature. It was only because Americans trusted Roosevelt as a genuine frontier hero that millions were willing to listen to him when he challenged America's frontier values. John Wesley Powell had been a genuine frontier hero in terms of undergoing an ordeal for the sake of western exploration, but Powell had overstepped the contract of American heroism. He had explored for science, not national expansion, and when he challenged national expansion in the name of science, warning of the West's aridity, he was slammed for it. Teddy Roosevelt's intense nationalism kept him within the code of national heroism and allowed him to challenge the national story of wilderness conquest. It was symbolic of the change of eras that only a few weeks after Powell died a defeated man, Roosevelt went on the bear hunt on which he refused to shoot a bear, giving rise to the teddy bear, which in the American imagination transformed bears from enemies of national expansion into symbols of a natural world that might deserve to be hugged.

Teddy Roosevelt was an unlikely person to become a cowboy or a hunter. He was the first US president born and raised in a big city (New York), and he lived in a mansion, went to Harvard, and did not need to work. As a boy he was undersized and underweight, suffered from severe asthma and digestive troubles, and could barely see without glasses. Eager to prove his toughness, he pursued an intense fitness agenda, which led to his fame as a hunter and a Rough Rider.

Teddy Roosevelt grew up loving stories about Wild West adventures, especially hunting. He killed his first deer at age fifteen. He longed to go to the Dakota Badlands, the last stronghold of the buffalo, and kill some before they were gone. When Teddy was twenty-six years old his mother and wife died on the same day, and he was so traumatized that he fled to the Badlands for most of the next three years to forget and recover.

Roosevelt showed up in the Badlands wearing tailored buckskin clothes with fringes, trying to look like Davy Crockett and Daniel Boone—the locals laughed at him. Teddy went on long hunting trips and killed elk, even knowing they were nearly the last elk in the Badlands. He wrote two best-selling books about his hunting adventures, which also made him famous as a rancher, for Roosevelt had bought two cattle ranches. When Roosevelt returned to New York City and ran for mayor in 1886, he proudly ran as "the Dakota cowboy."

Yet Roosevelt was also troubled by what he had seen in the West. He had

FIGURE 5.2. Former president Teddy Roosevelt (*right*) at Cliff Spring on the North Rim in 1913, on his mountain lion hunt. Roosevelt made the Grand Canyon a national monument in 1908.

arrived just in time to see the disappearance of America's once great herds of wildlife. He saw forests being clear-cut, grasslands being overgrazed, farm soils eroding, and mines pouring wastes into once beautiful streams. Roosevelt was troubled on several levels.

Roosevelt believed that the frontier had made Americans a great, heroic people, like Boone and Crockett. But now the frontier values Boone and Crockett had helped generate had become so omnivorous, they were destroying the forests and wildlife that had made Boone and Crockett great. Roosevelt himself had participated in this paradox by glorying in exterminating the Badlands' last elk and buffalo. Roosevelt worried that when the frontier was gone, Americans would experience only dirty cities and become a weak people. Roosevelt's personal need for vigorous outdoor adventure now became translated into the conviction that national vitality required wilderness and wildlife.

Roosevelt was also disturbed that much of the exploitation of the West was being done by Gilded Age corporations. Roosevelt was developing his progressive philosophy and saw conservation as part of it, another form of placing the common man and democratic values above privilege and private profits.

Most important, Teddy Roosevelt had absorbed America's long love of nature. In one of his books, *The Wilderness Hunter,* Roosevelt began by quoting Walt Whitman, and he praised the nature writers Burroughs and Thoreau. During these years Americans were still groping to translate their love of nature into a conservation ethic, but Roosevelt had already learned this ethic from his uncle Robert, a pioneering conservationist, and his father, one of the founders of the American Museum of Natural History, the charter for which was drawn up in the front room of the Roosevelt home.

The American love of nature had deep roots. In their Bibles Americans read a Genesis in which nature was a garden full of harmony, beauty, and sustenance. In their personal and national experience Americans saw their continent as a refuge from tyranny, a bountiful gift, and a chance to start human society over again in a more perfect form. America's founding fathers came of age reading Enlightenment philosophers who declared that nature was a rational, orderly Newtonian system and that human society should reflect this rationality. They read romantic philosophers like Rousseau, who had renewed the biblical image of nature as pure and harmonious; human society was the source of all corruption, and a better life and society could be found by "getting back to nature." For many romantics, including Americans such as Emerson and Thoreau, nature was also divine, a revelation of the mind of God, full of wisdom and peace. Although Enlightenment and romantic philosophers might argue about whether nature was Newtonian or an active divinity, America's founding fathers considered it the destiny of their nature-embedded nation to remake the world according to, in Jefferson's words, "the Laws of Nature and of Nature's God." As Americans developed their own culture, it was more nature oriented than European culture, which was more society oriented. America's heroes included explorers like Lewis and Clark and Daniel Boone. America generated nature seers like Thoreau and Whitman. America's most important novels were those dealing with the forces of nature: Cooper's Leatherstocking in the woods, Twain's Huck Finn on the river, Melville's Ahab on the sea.

Yet even in the 1820s, James Fenimore Cooper was worrying about overhunting and about lumber barons destroying forests. A half century later, in 1873, Mark Twain's first novel, *The Gilded Age,* which gave the name to its historical era, protested America becoming a colossus of greed. Eighteen years later Twain's coauthor of *The Gilded Age,* Charles Dudley Warner, became the first notable author to visit the Grand Canyon, and he wrote of his hope that the canyon might shock Americans into a sense of humility before nature.

What the United States really needed in the late 1800s was political leaders who could turn America's love of nature into a conservation ethic and into public policy. In 1872 there had been an important breakthrough: America had conceived the idea of national parks and made Yellowstone the world's first national park. Yet 1872 also brought the passage of the mining law that would give mining companies an iron grip on the land. Yellowstone was ahead of its time; nearly two decades of Wild West frenzy passed before Americans created another national park.

When Teddy Roosevelt returned from the Badlands to New York City, he began organizing his influential conservation-minded friends. With George Bird Grinnell he founded the Boone and Crockett Club, the first American organization for promoting conservation legislation; Roosevelt became its first president. They campaigned for better protection for Yellowstone National Park and opposed the building of a railroad through it. Roosevelt played a big role in the passage of the Forest Reserve Act of 1891, which allowed a president to set aside forests. It was good timing for the Grand Canyon, for in 1891 the president was Benjamin Harrison.

The year after Benjamin Harrison became a US senator from Indiana in 1881, he had introduced legislation to make the Grand Canyon a national park. When this effort was defeated by the protests of miners, loggers, and ranchers, Senator Harrison tried twice more, in 1883 and 1886, but these bills also failed. Benjamin Harrison's enthusiasm for the Grand Canyon is a bit mysterious, for he never visited it. Horace Albright, the second director of the NPS, once asked Benjamin Harrison's grandson William why Benjamin Harrison had been such a good conservationist, and William replied that he did not know. Then again, Albright met William Harrison because William was a park ranger at Yellowstone, so William may have inherited some family appreciation for nature. Benjamin Harrison was an outdoorsman, a hunter and fisherman, but not in the same league as Teddy Roosevelt. In 1881 Harrison visited Yellowstone in the company of artist Albert Bierstadt, and Harrison returned there in 1885. He did not like the idea of railroad corporations laying claim to national park land, so he introduced a bill to limit hotel development at Yellowstone to only ten acres.

The Forest Reserve Act of 1891 gave President Harrison the authority to create forest reserves, later to be called "national forests," and he created seventeen of them, including, on February 20, 1893, the Grand Canyon Forest Reserve. Harrison was stretching the Forest Reserve Act far beyond its intended purpose, for while the canyon rim held forests, most of the land he protected, the inner canyon, did not. Harrison was also tempted to use the Forest Reserve Act to protect Arizona's Petrified Forest, but his advisers told him this was ludicrous since the only forests there had died millions of years ago. The Grand Canyon Forest Reserve was weak protection, for it could not overrule existing mining and logging claims. It was supposed to curtail overgrazing, but ranchers flagrantly ignored the new rules, and enforcement was impractical. All it really achieved was to bar new homesteading. But the Grand Canyon Forest Reserve was the first of three levels of protection on the canyon's way to becoming a national park. The next two would be implemented by President Roosevelt. Like Harrison, Roosevelt would be so eager to protect the Grand Canyon that he would warp the law.

Benjamin Harrison was a conservationist too soon, before there was much of a constituency to support his efforts. Americans were enthralled by the Wild West, which was generating enormous national wealth, romantic myths, and businesses and tycoons with huge political clout. Most Americans accepted that western lands were meant for mining, logging, grazing, commercial hunting, and hydroelectric power. Yet quietly, behind the Wild West frenzy, conservation values were gathering strength.

With the ideas about nature they had inherited from the Enlightenment and romanticism, Americans had always had a good intellectual foundation for conservation values. But pioneers trying to survive on the frontier did not have much time for fancy ideas. As America prospered it generated a larger middle class, millions with college educations and the money to take vacations. As the United States became an urban nation, there were millions who missed the countryside; in various ways Americans cultivated a belief in the regenerative powers of nature. Affluent Americans had felt obligated to take their vacations in Europe, whose cities were far grander than American cities and whose natural landscapes, especially the Alps, were famous from European art and poetry. Now Americans were hearing that their western landscapes were more amazing than Europe's. These landscapes were taking a powerful grip on some of their first explorers and finding eloquent expression. John Wesley Powell was giving voice to the Grand Canyon. Thomas Moran was turning Yellowstone into brilliant paintings. John Muir was declaring that Yosemite was a cathedral greater than any human-made cathedral. These were also the decades when science was revealing geological eras and biological evolution, and people were seeing new depths in nature. Nature's vast, ancient story seemed to call for greater humility from humans. Nature's powers were displayed in the Grand Canyon better than anywhere else.

Americans were also realizing that their landscapes and wildlife were being destroyed, that human progress could bring big losses. Bountiful farmlands were eroding into gullies and stones. Magnificent forests and herds of buffalo had disappeared. Bird species were being wiped out so that ladies could wear fashionable feathers. Easterners were realizing that their mining stocks were financing scars on newly famous natural wonders.

Enthusiasm and worry for nature began generating political organizations and activity. Five years after Teddy Roosevelt cofounded the Boone and Crockett Club, John Muir founded the Sierra Club. But they remained voices in the wilderness compared with the Wild West and Gilded Age forces devoted to conquering the wilderness. In the thirty years between the creation of Yellowstone National Park and the presidency of Teddy Roosevelt, conservationists were having a tough time creating more national parks. Then conservationists found an unlikely but very powerful ally: the railroads.

In the 1880s John Muir and other conservationists were struggling to stop the destruction of the giant trees in the Sierra Nevada and to turn Yosemite and Sequoia into national parks. Muir was an eloquent advocate, yet money talked much louder than Muir. Then the Southern Pacific Railroad threw its considerable weight into the cause. In the Gilded Age the railroads were the most despised of the robber barons, and the Southern Pacific was one of the most notorious, the target of Frank Norris's 1901 muckraking novel, *The Octopus*—tourists riding Santa Fe trains to the Grand Canyon in 1901 were reading Norris's novel and feeling indignation against the evil railroads. Yet America's railroad executives were vacationing in Europe and seeing tourism thriving in the Alps, and they saw the possibilities for tourism in America's mountains. John Muir was astonished when, in 1890, the parks bill he had been pushing in Congress not only passed but created a Sequoia National Park much larger than he had asked for or dared hoped for. The Southern Pacific Railroad had been pulling political strings.

John Muir's attitude toward tourism and the railroads seems to have come from a premonition of the fate, a quarter of a century later, of Hetch Hetchy Valley, which was inside Yosemite National Park and the equal of Yosemite Valley yet got buried under a reservoir three hundred feet deep. While tourists had been visiting and falling in love with Yosemite Valley, Hetch Hetchy was a "place no one knew." It had no political constituency to defend it. The need for a constituency was a lesson conservationists learned painfully over and over; four decades after Hetch Hetchy was lost, even the Sierra Club acquiesced in the building of Glen Canyon Dam on the Colorado River and the flooding of Glen Canyon, which they later mourned with the book *The Place No One Knew.*

At heart John Muir was a purist who viewed Yosemite and the Grand Canyon as cathedrals in which to feel the presence of God; he probably would have preferred to throw the tourism money changers out of the temple. But if the money changers would help keep out the vandals, Muir would throw them his dollars. Muir wrote articles encouraging Yosemite tourism and rented himself out as a guide. He accepted the need for hotels and even favored building a road from Yosemite Valley into Hetch Hetchy. And Muir recognized that if you wanted tourists, you needed railroads.

John Muir struck up an unlikely friendship with Union Pacific Railroad tycoon Edward Harriman. In 1899 Muir sailed on Harriman's private steamboat on a cruise to Alaska. Muir and Harriman had a candid talk about their different values. Muir openly disapproved of Harriman's grasping for money and power and his bear hunting on their trip; Harriman tried to convince Muir that he genuinely appreciated nature. Muir set their differences aside and cultivated Harriman as an ally in the conservation movement, which did pay off when Harriman threw his political power into Muir's campaign to expand Yosemite National Park. When someone asked Harriman about Robert Stanton's plan to build a railroad through the Grand Canyon, Harriman branded it a "damned fool" idea.[1] A dozen years later Muir retreated to Harriman's private estate to write his memoirs.

Muir also had personal ties with the Santa Fe Railway. In 1897, for a token ten dollars, Muir sold the Santa Fe a right-of-way through his own ranch. The Santa Fe built a viaduct over Muir's vineyards and set up "Muir Station," which allowed Muir to ship his produce to market more efficiently. Muir would ride the Santa Fe into San Francisco to hold a Sierra Club meeting and plan resistance against industrial development and then ride home in time for dinner. In 1902 Muir took the newly opened Santa Fe line to the Grand Canyon. In an article Muir wrote for a national magazine he admitted he had had misgivings about the railroad reaching the canyon rim, but he declared, "In the presence of such stupendous scenery they are nothing. The locomotives and trains are mere beetles and caterpillars, and the noise they make is as little disturbance as the hooting of an owl in the lonely woods."[2]

If President Roosevelt read Muir's words, he must have been appalled. Roosevelt never would have hung out with Edward Harriman, whom he despised. In 1902 Roosevelt used antitrust laws to break up Harriman's railroad empire, a major victory that frightened all the robber barons. Roosevelt regarded the railroads not as owls but as vampires, and he hated the idea of their getting their fangs on the national parks. Roosevelt was appalled to learn that at the Grand Canyon, Santa Fe Railway thugs were carrying guns and herding tourists in their power struggle against Ralph Cameron. But he was not surprised, since he regarded railroad presidents as bigger thugs.

In 1903 Roosevelt took a long train trip around the West, and he visited Yosemite and went tramping with John Muir. Roosevelt and Muir, the big-game hunter and the nature mystic, did not entirely understand one another, but they recognized their common cause. Roosevelt also visited the Grand Canyon. He was, of course, riding on the tracks and the trains of the robber barons. On May 6, 1903, Roosevelt stood on the porch of the Bright Angel Hotel, which was affiliated with the Santa Fe Railway, and he took dead aim at the Santa Fe, which was planning to build a luxury hotel, El Tovar, and other facilities on the rim. To Roosevelt, this was vandalism. Roosevelt apparently had the mistaken idea that these plans had been canceled, and he declared:

> I was delighted to learn of the wisdom of the Santa Fe Railroad in deciding not to build their hotel on the brink of the cañon. I hope you will not have a building of any kind, not a summer cottage, a hotel or anything else, to mar the wonderful grandeur, sublimity, the great loneliness and beauty of the cañon.

Leave it as it is. You cannot improve on it; not a bit. The ages have been at work on it, and man can only mar it. What you can do is to keep it for your children, your children's children and for all who come after you, as one of the great sites which every American, if he can travel at all, should see. Keep the Grand Cañon as it is.[3]

After both President Harrison and President Roosevelt had expressed opposition to letting railroads get a grip on national parks, this might have settled the question. But in the end, John Muir's attitude was more politically strategic. President Roosevelt's speech had contained a hopeless contradiction: he wanted every American, all eighty million of them, to rush to the Grand Canyon, but he also wanted to see no trace of humans there. Today Roosevelt's speech has become an iconic statement of the values and purpose of the National Park Service, frequently quoted by park rangers all over the country, but rangers almost always omit the part about not allowing any hotels or other buildings in national parks.

John Muir and Teddy Roosevelt approached the question of tourism and development in national parks from sharply different backgrounds. Muir, the son of a poor farmer, had been a wilderness tramp who felt powerless against the juggernaut of the Wild West and the Gilded Age, and he sought to win converts among the powerful. Teddy Roosevelt, the son of an aristocratic family, had always had a brash, forceful personality, and now he was president of the United States and he expected to get his way, especially because he had no doubt of his moral superiority. The contrasting attitudes of Muir and Roosevelt defined a dilemma, a conflict over values and purpose, which the NPS is still struggling with today.

Stephen Mather, who in 1916 became the first director of the National Park Service, idolized John Muir and accepted Muir's attitude about the need to build a political constituency for the national parks, millions of people who cared about natural wonders because they had been there. At the start of the twentieth century, when most Americans lived in the East and all national parks were in the West, the only way to have tourism was to have railroads and park hotels. Mather committed the NPS to a philosophy of commercial and other development in parks that would remain strong for more than a half century, until its paradoxes became too painful.

Of course, by the time Stephen Mather came along, the partnership between the railroads and the national parks was well established, and

FIGURE 5.3. Car on canyon rim, 1914. Early NPS leaders felt tourism was essential for conservation victories. But at what point does tourism become just another environmental threat?

Mather simply went along with it. The Santa Fe Railway arrived at the Grand Canyon seven years before it became a national monument, eighteen years before it became a national park, and fifteen years before there was any National Park Service. This delay might have been even longer, but the railroads were campaigning for the creation of new national parks and of a National Park Service. When the NPS started out, it was a small and badly underfunded agency that faced very powerful opponents, and it was grateful to have an ally strong enough to do battle against mining corporations, US senators, and private inholders like Ralph Cameron.

In its first year the Santa Fe Railway brought more tourists to the Grand Canyon than had seen it in all previous years combined. The Santa Fe spent a lot of money promoting the canyon. They latched on to a trend among America's cultural leaders, an idea summarized by the slogan "See America First." European cities and art might be superior to American cities and art, but American nature was superior to any European cathedral and in fact superior to European nature. Why go see the Matterhorn when you could see the Grand Canyon? This "America first" trend was probably reinforced by the isolationist mood of Americans after World War I, when Europe seemed less admirable. An ascendant America was feeling proud of itself, and its natural wonders seemed grand enough to be icons of national pride. National identity is a powerful force, ready to latch on to anything that serves it, even a canyon that proclaimed the transience and vanity of all nations. Yet in the same year—1919—that Mussolini and Hitler were drawing upon ancient military glories and domination fantasies to stoke the fires of pathological nationalism, Americans celebrated their nationalism by creating Grand Canyon National Park.

Teddy Roosevelt became president twenty years after Benjamin Harrison had first tried to make the Grand Canyon a national park, and now Roosevelt took up the cause. The conservation movement had been growing, and so had support for national parks. But there was nothing inevitable about the conservation triumphs of the Roosevelt years; far less would have happened if William McKinley had remained president. Social trends were less important than Roosevelt's forceful personality. If Congress was not interested in conservation, Roosevelt would get results through presidential proclamations. He proclaimed 152 national forests and 51 bird reservations—now called national wildlife refuges. But national parks could not be created by presidential decree; they required an act of Congress. Roosevelt got Congress to go along with several national parks, but none held significant natural resources or powerful private owners. The Grand Canyon did. Arizona politicians and business leaders were still denouncing national parks as un-American, and their opposition carried a lot of weight with Congress.

Congress was willing to protect a few thousand deer on the canyon's North Rim, and on November 28, 1906, Roosevelt signed a bill creating the Grand Canyon Game Preserve—where soon Jimmy Owens was slaughtering all predators. Teddy Roosevelt may have been a visionary conservationist, but for him and for science itself the idea of ecosystems was barely on the map.

In 1913, after his presidency, Teddy went to the North Rim and joined Jimmy Owens to hunt mountain lions. Roosevelt: "It was a wild sight. The maddened hounds bayed at the foot of the pine. Above them, in the lower branches, stood the big horse-killing cat, the destroyer of the deer, the lord of stealthy murder, facing his doom with a heart both craven and cruel. Almost beneath him the vermillion cliffs fell sheer a thousand feet

without a break. Behind him lay the Grand Canyon in its awful and desolate majesty."[4]

Roosevelt could now look at the canyon with double pride, for he had
bagged his canyon political prey, too. On June 6, 1906, President Roosevelt
signed the Antiquities Act, spearheaded though Congress by Iowa congressman John Lacey. Lacey was fascinated by the Southwest's Indian ruins
and wanted to defend them from looters. He drafted a bill that created a
new class of public lands called national monuments, to protect archaeological sites and "historic preservation structures, and other objects of scientific interest." Lacey wrote the law so subtly that Congress did not realize
how much power it was giving away to the president, who got sole authority to declare national monuments. In less than three years Roosevelt
created eighteen national monuments. Of the first five, three were major
archaeological sites, such as Chaco Canyon. But the first five also included
the Petrified Forest, which did have a few good archaeological sites, but
these were small dots in a vast landscape of badlands and petrified logs.
Luckily, the Grand Canyon too had ruins. And like petrified logs, the canyon's geology could be called "other objects of scientific interest."

It is not clear why Roosevelt waited a year and a half, until January 11,
1908, to declare the Grand Canyon a national monument. Perhaps he felt
that the canyon deserved to be a national park and that mere monument
status was beneath its dignity. He was also hoping that Arizonans would
trade the Grand Canyon for statehood, which Arizonans had been seeking for a long time and would not win until 1912. He also knew that his
broad interpretation of the Antiquities Act would provoke outrage and
legal challenges. Indeed, his designation of Grand Canyon National Monument brought a lawsuit that went on for years and went all the way to the
US Supreme Court. In 1920 the Supreme Court agreed that Grand Canyon
rocks held "scientific interest."

The national monument held 1,279 square miles, including the most
scenic areas being enjoyed by tourists, but it included only 105 miles of
the Grand Canyon's 277 miles (as measured by the Colorado River). Monument status stopped further mining claims, but it could not remove existing claims—if they were valid. Very slowly, the government began assaying
mining claims and invalidating the ones without ore, claims filed merely
to control the tourism business. There was still no National Park Service,
so administration of the monument was left in the hands of the Forest

Service, and it remained there until the park was established in 1919. But the Forest Service was more experienced at managing resource extraction than resource protection or tourist services, and it had little funding and manpower to manage the monument. Its Grand Canyon headquarters consisted of a ten-by-twelve-foot tent house. The Forest Service now considered the Grand Canyon to be the crown jewel of its system, the best place for it to impress the American public. This made the Forest Service opposed to making the canyon a national park, and indeed it opposed the creation of a National Park Service, which would be a bureaucratic turf rival.

Theodore Roosevelt left office regretting that, amid all his accomplishments, he had failed to get the Grand Canyon made into a national park. He was baffled that Americans did not seem to see the canyon's greatness. Then he headed off to the canyon's North Rim to blast away at mountain lions and thrill in the bloody glory of the Wild West.

CHAPTER SIX

Culture
Pioneers of Perception

In the same decades the Grand Canyon was caught in a conflict over how Americans viewed their land, it was also immersed in a larger cultural confusion. Science was revolutionizing how humans viewed the universe and themselves.

In 1869, the year John Wesley Powell struggled down the Colorado River, Dmitry Mendeleyev published the first periodic table of the elements. In 1905, the year El Tovar Hotel opened, Albert Einstein published his relativity theory. In 1912, the year Grand Canyon photographers Emery and Ellsworth Kolb turned their motion down the Colorado River into a motion picture, Alfred Wegener proposed that the continents were moving. In 1919, the year Grand Canyon became a national park, Edwin Hubble began the work that would prove that the universe is expanding. In July 1925, the year the park hired geologist Glen Sturdevant as its first ranger-naturalist, the Scopes Trial had turned the teaching of evolution into a national debate.

Science was revealing an Earth billions of years old, its fossil-rich rocks made out of a long procession of evolving species, in a universe of billions of outrushing galaxies. For many people, this universe could be dizzying. Cultural leaders were debating science and its implications. This was the peak of social Darwinism, which was being used to justify war, racism, extreme inequality, and Gilded Age capitalism—including railroad monopolies. Writers Mark Twain, Jack London, Theodore Dreiser, Henry Adams, and Frank Norris were weighing in with major works on science, religion, and social Darwinism.

Scientific ideas could seem like abstractions, but at the Grand Canyon ideas about deep time and primordial forces could suddenly leap into a powerfully real manifestation. Yet in the first years of canyon tourism, many visitors found the canyon deeply disturbing. The comments of early visitors, including some of America's most prominent poets and writers, are loaded with expressions of shock, dismay, and outright horror. Some of this shock arose because visitors in 1901 had not seen innumerable images of the canyon. Charles Lummis, the leading advocate for the Southwest, wrote in 1902, "I have seen people rave over it; better people struck dumb with it; even strong men who cried over it; but I have never yet seen the man or woman who *expected* it."[1] Some of this shock was aesthetic, the same shock Americans expressed at New York's 1913 Armory Show when they got their first look at modern art; the Grand Canyon was a Picasso or van Gogh of landscapes. Some of this shock was in accord with the romantic idea of the sublime, which allowed for a fearful reaction to a landscape—but a reaction that was still one of humility before God's power. Yet some of this shock came from people unable to even recognize the sublime, people discovering they lived on a bizarre new planet. For some visitors, the canyon assaulted their sense of reality and personal identity and triggered existential vertigo.

Such philosophical dizziness was felt by Henry Van Dyke, a clergyman who had chaired the committee that wrote the first Presbyterian liturgy and a widely popular poet of Christian themes. At the canyon Van Dyke had a vision of human insignificance. In the title poem of his 1914 book, *The Grand Canyon,* Van Dyke saw humans as

> a conscious grain of sand
> Lost in a desert of unconsciousness
> Thirsting for God and mocked by his own thirst.

Van Dyke felt "the fathomless abyss" drawing him toward suicide. But then his religious impulses began fighting back, trying to absorb this new reality onto a Christian template, and he ends the poem by telling the canyon: "If God were blind thy Beauty could not be!"[2]

It was ironic that Henry Van Dyke used desert imagery as a symbol of meaninglessness, for a decade previously his cousin John C. Van Dyke had published *The Desert,* which challenged such negative images and insisted that deserts were beautiful and inspiring. In 1920 John C. Van Dyke wrote a book about the Grand Canyon and devoted a whole chapter to figuring out "the terror of the abyss," why people (like cousin Henry) could find the canyon so disturbing. John C. Van Dyke studied a Hopi standing right on the rim, "with no feeling of fear and not the slightest thought about suicide or insanity." For the Hopis, the canyon was sacred and home. Van Dyke saw civilization as insane, so disconnected from nature that the real universe came as a shock. "But there is no madness in Nature and no terror in her precipices once we have the fumes of civilization out of our brain." John refused to follow Henry in trying to turn the Grand Canyon into a Christian testament. For John, the ultimate reality is nature, and human smallness before nature's mystery inspires not terror but a nourishing wonder. John closes his book by saying that the canyon "is too big for us to do more than creep along the Rim and wonder over it. Perhaps that is not cause for lamentation. . . . The mystery that surrounds her should remain a mystery. As for our wonder, it is a natural inheritance. We opened our eyes upon the world with awe and we close them at the last groping our way in starry spaces. May it never cease!"[3]

As it was for Henry and John C. Van Dyke, the Grand Canyon would serve as rich raw material for a generation of poets, writers, artists, and everyday tourists who were trying to come to terms with the new realities of science.

The "terror of the abyss" was exacerbated because many visitors were expecting to find beauty, but the canyon held a visual language that most visitors found hard to read. In romantic paintings and poetry beauty had never been a matter of mere aesthetics, of pretty scenery; it was a symbol of divinity. For Thoreau and Muir, the beauty of Walden or Yosemite said that the ultimate reality of the cosmos was wise and sacred. Walden and Yosemite had worked perfectly well as traditional romantic landscapes, but the Grand Canyon and the desert Southwest did not. John C. Van Dyke had realized this with a shock when in 1897 he developed severe asthma and his doctor ordered him to retreat to the desert. The desert dismayed him, for it violated every aesthetic rule in the art history books he had written, every definition of natural beauty. It held little life and no water, only bare, weird rocks, and its light was raw and glaring. The desert was skeletal, decayed, elemental. Yet as the desert began restoring his health, John began feeling that "elemental" might actually be good. Van Dyke became obsessed with the desert, risked his life to explore it, and wrote *The Desert* to justify why the desert, taken on its own terms, was beautiful and nourishing.

John C. Van Dyke was way ahead of the tourists arriving at the Grand Canyon in 1901. Their hopes for seeing beauty were answered with some strange and downright negative signals. The link to divinity had been snatched away.

Early reactions to the canyon can be gauged most tellingly by the 1902 book *The Grand Canyon of Arizona,* a compilation of many authors, which the Santa Fe Railway intended as a promotional device. As such, it is a strange document. It is full of gloom and outright terror. Three authors reported suicidal impulses. This included C. S. Gleed, who was on the Santa Fe's board of directors. Gleed saw that "the pit was bottomless—the grave of the world.... A paralysis of surprise held us. Helplessness wound about us ... the void beckoned. We scarcely knew why we did not obey the summons." This was an odd way to sell tickets. C. A. Higgins, who was in charge of the Santa Fe's advertising, wrote, "Stolid indeed is he who can font the awful scene ... without quaking knee or tremulous breath." George Reeve, vice president of the Grand Trunk Railroad, wrote, "The Grand Canyon. What is it? I do not know; you do not know; God only knows."[4]

William Allen White, the Kansas newspaper editor and Republican Party statesman, did not admit suicidal impulses but seemed to understand them:

> It is the silence of the place that appalls.... Indeed, the spirit of the thing below seems to creep into a man's soul through his body and lay hold upon his heart and nerves. At night, as he lies in his bed, the terrific depths that strained his eyes by day reach up and grapple him. There is a lift and mass about these walls that fills the soul with unutterable things.... Moonlight in the canyon is a ghastly sight; the life goes out of the light, and one seems to be looking upon the face of death.... At night the silence of the stars and the silence of this pit— each eternal and maddening to human consciousness—mingle in an awful spell that falls upon the soul like the lonesomeness of the grave.[5]

The authors in *The Grand Canyon of Arizona* did not talk much about beauty. Of the book's forty-nine authors, fewer than a third of them ever mentioned the words *beauty* or *beautiful*. This was partly because they were having a hard time recognizing beauty in the canyon and partly because they were seeking something deeper than aesthetics, something primordial. William Allen White explained, "One should not say that the canyon is beautiful; it transcends mere beauty and passes into a 'far more exceeding glory.' ... He is in the presence of big, simple, primordial things that go to the core of human nature, and seeing these things man may not babble of matters frescoed on the surface of life.... No one has ever carried away ... on a canvas, even a true hint of it."[6]

The book included some of President Teddy Roosevelt's 1903 words at the canyon (not, of course, his tirade against the Santa Fe Railway), and

Teddy had not made any campaign promises about beauty, only that the canyon "fills me with awe." Among the authors who did speak of beauty, this beauty could be strange and tortured. For John Muir, it was "the natural beauty of desolation and death."[7]

The book contained numerous gloomy images. Reverend C. B. Spencer of Denver saw "Horror! Tragedy! Silence! Death! Chaos! There is the awful canyon in five words. . . . It seemed to me as if it were the burying ground of the universe. It is the delirium of Nature. . . . The mind at first stands aghast. There is a sense of terror that cannot be put into words." Famous travel lecturer John L. Stoddard saw "Nature wounded unto death and lying stiff and ghastly. . . . I felt as if I were the sole survivor of the deluge. Only the melancholy murmur of the wind ascended that sepulchre of centuries. It seemed the requiem for a vanished world." Novelist Charles Dudley Warner "experienced for a moment an indescribable terror of nature, a confusion of mind, a fear to be alone in such a presence. With all this grotesqueness and majesty of form and radiance of color, creation seemed a whirl."[8]

One of the contributors who described a suicidal impulse at the canyon was Chicago poet Harriet Monroe. Like John C. Van Dyke, she came to the desert only when forced by illness, and she struggled to adjust her perceptions. From her convalescent chair in Phoenix, she studied the desert's shapes and light, and she decided that it, as she recalled in her autobiography, "had a weird and hoary beauty of its own, very unlike the beauty of green fields and thick forests but quite as potent. It seemed the most ancient thing on earth. It suggested immensities of time. . . . Gradually I felt convinced of entering another world, accepting unfamiliar laws. . . . Humanity had no rights in this enormous desolation; I intruded upon its profound mysterious beauty."[9]

It was this sense of intruding upon an ancient and alien realm that triggered Monroe's existential panic at the Grand Canyon, an emotional reaction too powerful for her to absorb. She described it in the Santa Fe's book: "I intruded here. Everywhere the proof of my unfitness abased and dazed my will. . . . The strain of existence became too tense against these infinities of beauty and terror. My narrow ledge of rock was a prison. I fought against the desperate temptation to fling myself down into that soft abyss, and thus redeem the affront which the beating of my eager heart offered to its inviolable solitude. Death itself would not be too rash an apology for my invasion."[10] In spite of this experience—or because of it—the canyon became Monroe's "house of dreams." She returned to the canyon many times, hiked and camped in it, and was enthralled by its power.

In 1912 Harriet Monroe founded *Poetry* magazine in Chicago; *Poetry* closed the long, stale Victorian era in American poetry and made Monroe the midwife of modern poetry. Her circle of poets (which included Chicago's Carl Sandburg and Edgar Lee Masters) knew of her fascination with the Grand Canyon, and they began writing Grand Canyon poems. The third issue of *Poetry* included "At the Grand Canyon" by George Sterling, who had become one of the best-known American poets of the time by grappling with the new scientific universe, offering a mostly nihilistic response. Now he did the same for the Grand Canyon, echoing Monroe in saying, "Here Terror walks with Beauty."[11]

Some of Monroe's poets were readier to see divinity in the Grand Canyon. In 1920 Monroe received a letter from Sara Teasdale, who was visiting the canyon and having an intense experience. "It makes me feel," wrote Teasdale, "that immortality must Be, after all, since the ages have worked for such harmonious splendor there."[12] Alfred Noyes was a British poet whom Monroe recruited for *Poetry* in its first year, and he would write a 328-page epic poem, *The Book of Earth,* to justify the Grand Canyon as a Christian landscape. For Noyes, the answer was not the creationist project of shrinking the scientific cosmos into the seven-day scale of biblical creation, but expanding God to be as big as Hubble's cosmos.

Noyes begins *The Book of Earth* on the canyon rim at night. In a section called "Night and the Abyss," he faces, like Harriet Monroe, a vision of a canyon and cosmos that are a spiritual abyss, and he wonders if all we can hope for, like John C. Van Dyke, is that *"Man must bow his head before the Inscrutable."*[13] He asks for a deeper vision, hoping to see canyon and cosmos glowing with God's glory. Watching a moth fluttering out over the canyon, he sees:

> Brave little fluttering atheist, unaware
> Of aught beyond the reach of his antennae,
> Thinking his light quick Thoughts; while
>   under him,
> God opened His immeasurable Abyss.[14]

Noyes leads a 300-page journey through the ideas of geology and biology, meeting seers like Leonardo and Goethe and especially Darwin, and then he returns to the Grand Canyon and concludes that the Book of Earth is really God's scripture written in stone. To a canyon sunrise, he concludes, "New every morning the creative Word moves upon chaos."[15]

Carl Sandburg, discovered by Harriet Monroe, was mainly known for his populist vision of America, but he also loved nature. Sandburg wrote two long poems, "Slabs of the Sunburnt West" and "Many Hats," that used the Grand Canyon to calibrate the meaning of the scientific cosmos and the location of God in it. Sandburg refers to Monroe's experience at the canyon: "Why did one woman cry, The silence is / terrible? Why did another smile, There is sweet gravity here?"[16]

In the canyon rocks, Sandburg feels:

The power and lift of the sea
and the flame of the old earth fires under,
I sift their meanings of sand in my fingers.
I send out five sleepwalkers to find out who I am,
my name and number, where I came from,
and where I am going.[17]

Sandburg can never figure it out. He is ready to find God in the canyon, but God eludes him: "How can I touch with my fingers a fingerless God? . . . Or look on a God who never needs eyes for looking?"[18] Sandburg ends up simply observing all the answers that other people, from Hopis to cowboys, have found in the canyon. He concludes:

For each man sees him—
self in the Grand Canyon—
each one makes his own Canyon
before he comes, each one brings
and carries away his own Canyon.[19]

Today this Sandburg quote is engraved on the wall of the park's Visitor Center auditorium, where visitors contemplate it while waiting for the park's introductory film to begin. Then they head for the canyon rim and create still more canyons.

It was not just poets who were trying to figure out the meaning of the canyon. During its first decade El Tovar Hotel offered guests a journal in which they recorded their efforts to fit the canyon into their ideas about natural wonders, beauty, religion, and science. A few people had trouble seeing the canyon as beautiful, one writing, "Lifeless, supporting no life in its terrifying depths, the Grand Canyon repels me beyond expression. I can see nothing but its desolation and waste."[20] But most people found it "sublime" or "beautiful." About one out of six guests made comments attributing the canyon to either God or nature, and of those 78 percent gave the credit to God. The canyon was "God's autograph on nature's page," and it "ranks next to the Incarnation itself as a revelation of God." Skeptics wrote things like: "This natural phenomenon is certainly far greater than our wildest imaginings regarding the works of any divinity." Sometimes Christians and skeptics broke into open debate. After a skeptic wrote, "Truly wonderful, but only a ditch on a large scale. Water, earth, rock and time are the forces at work, and that have always worked. It is foolish to talk as if it is a work of God, Infinite, etc.," several believers wrote retorts, including calling the author an "idiot." After a Christian declared it "Throne of the Infinite!" a skeptic asked, "Would you put Him in a hole?" After a wife wrote, "A Masterpiece by the Great Architect of the Universe," her husband answered, "A Grand, Awful, and Peculiar Masterpiece of Nature's two most powerful elements, Fire and Water."

The canyon's refusal to fit cultural images of natural beauty created a dilemma for artists who set out to paint the canyon. People expected art to be beautiful. For the most important artist in Grand Canyon history, Thomas Moran, the solution was to ignore the real canyon and to impose onto it the habits of European landscape painting.

Thomas Moran was born in England in 1837, and English landscape painting would define his own style. He was especially enthralled with J. M. W. Turner; in his twenties Moran traveled around Europe, found the exact spot from which Turner had painted a scene, and painted the same scene with the same golden palette Turner had used. Moran settled in New York City in the heyday of the Hudson River School, which was applying European styles to American scenes. In 1871, after Moran had become a respected illustrator for *Scribner's* magazine, he was invited to serve as illustrator for the Hayden expedition to Yellowstone, still a vaguely known place. Thomas Moran painted a gigantic Yellowstone painting, twelve feet long and seven feet high, which the US Congress purchased for ten thousand dollars and hung in the Capitol.

John Wesley Powell was impressed, and he invited Moran to serve as illustrator on his further explorations, by land, of the Grand Canyon region

FIGURE 6.1. Artist Thomas Moran on Bright Angel Trail, ca. 1909.

in 1873. As Moran traveled through Utah toward the canyon, he was not admiring the landscapes. "It is an awful country," he wrote his wife, "that we have been traveling over and I cannot conceive how human beings can stand to live on it." But then, "On reaching the brink the whole gorge for miles lay beneath us and it was by far the most awfully grand and impressive scene that I have ever yet seen." Moran made the canyon his life's work, returning there for a half century, spending two entire winters there, painting and drawing it hundreds of times. His first was *The Chasm of the Colorado,* painted in 1873–74, the same size as his Yellowstone painting; Congress spent another ten thousand dollars for it and hung it in the Capitol, too. For the next quarter century far more Americans saw Thomas Moran's painting than saw the real canyon. As much as John Wesley Powell, Moran made the canyon famous. Yet in spite of Moran's concessions to public expectations of beauty, some viewers still found his canyon repulsive. *Scribner's* complained about "an oppressive wildness that weighs down the senses. . . . This seems to be a glimpse of another planet."[21]

Thomas Moran imposed onto the canyon the same golden look that J. M. W. Turner had given to the Italian countryside. When Moran gave one of his canyon sketches to famous art critic John Ruskin, Ruskin assumed it had been done by Turner and resisted Moran's assurances that it was his own work. This golden look had been legitimate for Yellowstone, which of course was named for its volcanic yellows, but with the Grand Canyon Moran was censoring what, to later generations of artists, would be the canyon's main aesthetic glory, its bands of many colors. Moran barely acknowledged the existence of geological strata. The real canyon is a strongly horizontal landscape, with layer upon layer running for dozens of miles, even through all the inner-canyon peaks. Moran turned the canyon into a vertical landscape, defined by all the peaks pointing skyward, like the Alps. Moran did not try to portray a real vista but invented his own, arranging both real and imaginary cliffs, peaks, and horizons to make a more pleasing composition. Moran filled the canyon with mist, which does happen occasionally during summer thunderstorms, but it was also a romantic convention for invoking the "mystical." Moran added sunbursts and a rainbow, also standard romantic symbols for divinity. Moran's canyon made geological forces and epochs safe and beautiful.

Because almost no one had seen the Grand Canyon in 1873, no one was going to know the difference between Moran's painting and the real thing. But after large numbers of tourists began arriving in 1901, Moran allowed more realistic strata and colors into his paintings, though he retained much of his 1873 look.

Moran's journeys to the canyon were sponsored by the Santa Fe Railway, which became a patron of dozens of artists. Some, like George Inness Jr., were already prominent, while others were young and getting their first big chance. The Santa Fe provided studio space on the rim, purchased hundreds of canyon paintings for its own collection, and opened a gallery in El Tovar for the public. Starving artists could trade paintings for room and board. The founders of the new Taos art colony came, including Ernest Blumenschein, Oscar Berninghaus, E. Irving Couse, and Walter Ufer. From Santa Fe came Gustave Baumann, Warren E. Rollins, Louis Hovey Sharp, and Gerald Cassidy. Some artists declared the canyon to be "an artist's nightmare" and never came back, but some young artists such as William R. Leigh, Carl Oscar Borg, and Louis Akin became so enthralled by the canyon that they arranged their lives to paint it and the Southwest.

Louis Akin became the first artist to live at the canyon for an extended period; he painted it about thirty-five times. He first came to the Southwest to paint the Hopis, whose culture rejuvenated his spirits from life in New York City (Akin's studio was across the street from the house where Teddy Roosevelt was born). Akin wanted to set up an artist colony on the Hopi mesas, but he was able to recruit only one artist, Kate Cory, who would soon be one of the first women artists to paint the Grand Canyon. In 1906 Akin did a painting of El Tovar and Hopi House, with the canyon plunging beneath them, which was widely reproduced by the Santa Fe Railway. It was one of the most blatantly promotional of canyon paintings, showing Hopi House much closer to the rim than it actually was; deleting the Santa Fe's rival store, Verkamp's; and adding a picturesque Hopi woman carrying a baby and a man riding a white horse. Yet Akin did not earn enough money from this painting to pay off his starving-artist debts. The next year Akin painted *Evening—Grand Canyon,* a Moran-scaled nine feet by six feet. Akin failed to sell it, so he kept it for the rest of his life, and it ended up on the wall of Verkamp's, the store he had deleted from his most famous painting. Akin remained poor and died of pneumonia in 1913 at age forty-five.

Akin painted the canyon more realistically than Thomas Moran, even as he was influenced by impressionism, which emphasized light and color and emotional impacts. This was a tumultuous time in the art world, with new styles pouring out of Europe and quickly arriving, through European artists, at the Grand Canyon. Yet romanticism was refusing to yield without a fight. For a while the most popular Grand Canyon artist was Elliot Daingerfield, whose 1913 *The Genius of the Grand Canyon* sold for fifteen thousand dollars, by far the highest price for any canyon painting thus far. Typical of Daingerfield's paintings, *Genius* showed a classical naked goddess posing on the canyon rim, while behind her the canyon peaks morphed into a dreamlike, heavenly city. The New Mexico artists could be tempted by the romantic convention of posing a mythic figure before a landscape, but their figures were Native Americans. These artists had moved to New Mexico because they were fascinated by Native Americans and their spirituality, so for them the Native figures implied that the Grand Canyon was a primal, spiritual landscape. For other artists, especially Americans, the posed mythic figures were cowboys. These human figures were there partly to give a sense of scale to a puzzling landscape, but they also made the Grandiose Canyon seem more approachable, a human domain. But Georgia O'Keeffe, who preferred more intimate landscapes, never felt like painting the canyon.

To this day artists are divided between painting the canyon in realistic or impressionistic styles, with most falling—or failing—on one side or the other. Some artists become so diligent at recording the canyon's shapes that they forgo its magical luminosity. Other artists emphasize light and color so much that the real cliffs become a blur.

In the 1920s the canyon attracted an artist who would solve this dilemma and become a model for artists ever since. He would be the only artist to join Thomas Moran in getting a rim overlook named for him. Gunnar Widforss, born in Sweden in 1879, was traveling across America to San Francisco, intending to sail for Asia, but Yosemite captured him. His paintings of Yosemite captured NPS director Stephen Mather, who organized a one-man National Gallery show of Widforss's national park scenes. When Widforss discovered the Grand Canyon he was enthralled, and he spent large portions of the next dozen years there and painted it more than two hundred times. He got to know the canyon better than most previous artists; he hiked to the canyon bottom and all over the rims, studying how the canyon light varied through the hours and the seasons. He painted with great accuracy and small details, but he also gave cliffs and trees a lyrical glow. He never posed human figures in his paintings, which were always about the canyon itself. His artist friends complained that Widforss's realism was out of step with an art world that was encouraging imagination, but Widforss pointed at the canyon and declared that imagination did not get any wilder than this. In 1934 a doctor warned Widforss that the canyon's high elevation was not good for his heart, so Widforss sadly packed his things and was leaving the canyon—when he had a heart attack and died. He was buried in the South Rim's Pioneer Cemetery, where today his admirers stick paint brushes onto his grave.

In the same decades that canyon art was evolving from Moran to Widforss, from evasion to realistic lyricism, nature writers like John Muir and John Burroughs were trying to adjust their perceptions. Unlike the poets who were using the canyon to test their sense of reality, Muir and Burroughs accepted nature as a meaningful foundation for human lives. Yet they too

FIGURE 6.2. Artist Gunnar Widforss painting on the canyon rim, 1925.

felt out of their element at the canyon. Muir puzzled over the "strange, leafless, old-fashioned plants . . . making the strangest forests ever seen or dreamed of." Burroughs mentioned Harriet Monroe's existential vertigo and seemed to be thinking of it in saying, "One's sense of the depths of the cañon is so great that it almost makes one dizzy to see the little birds fly over it, or plunge down into it. One seemed to fear that they, too, would get dizzy and fall to the bottom." Yet both writers then rose to the challenge of seeing geological grandeur. Muir was a more lyrical writer than Burroughs and less shy about finding God in nature and the canyon: "It seems a gigantic statement for even nature to make, all in one mighty stone word. . . . Wildness so godful, cosmic, primeval, bestows a new sense of earth's beauty and size. Not even from high mountains does the world seem so wide, so like a star in glory of light on its way through the heavens."[22]

Years later John C. Van Dyke and Mary Austin came to the canyon with desert-trained eyes and scorned writers—including Muir—who saw canyon landscapes as fanciful castles. Van Dyke saw the canyon mainly through aesthetic eyes and Austin through Native American eyes, once again proving Carl Sandburg's statement that everyone finds their own Grand Canyon.

John Muir and Stephen Mather had calculated that to turn natural wonders into national parks, wonders needed to be loved by a lot of people. As the Grand Canyon waited for decades (until 1919), a dozen other places, including Yosemite, Mount Rainier, and Rocky Mountain, leaped past it to become national parks. All those places were better fits for cultural images of natural beauty and sacred symbolism. Was the Grand Canyon slowed down not just because of Wild West values that saw the land as an economic resource, but because the canyon was initially seen as ugly and profane? This is impossible to measure, but it does fit the cultural time line. As the Grand Canyon waited, cultural leaders were immersing themselves in southwestern landscapes, struggling to interpret them, and expanding their definitions of natural beauty and meaning. Reactions of dismay were becoming much less common. Americans were becoming much more self-confident as a nation, and this meant taking more pride in their own land and being less subservient to European cultural habits. In 1919 American jazz and American writers such as T. S. Eliot were ready to become the world's voices, and Georgia O'Keeffe had launched a career that would seek inspiration not in Paris but in New Mexico. For the Grand Canyon, 1919 seems not just a political threshold, but a cultural one. In 1923 Gunnar Widforss arrived at the canyon and began painting it honestly, and in 1926 Ferde Grofé felt "an irresistible impulse" to begin his *Grand Canyon Suite*.[23]

Ferde Grofé first came to Arizona at age twenty-five, during World War I, when he volunteered as a musician in the US cavalry band. For years to come he returned to Arizona and visited the Grand Canyon. One time he rose in the dark to watch the sun rise over the canyon and was so astonished that he could not express it in words, but he heard the colors musically. In 1924 Grofé became famous for arranging a new George Gershwin composition for jazz piano into a work for full orchestra, the version of "Rhapsody in Blue" the world knows today. Convinced that only American music could do justice to American landscapes, Grofé drew upon jazz to attempt a Grand Canyon rhapsody. Its most famous section, depicting the clip-clopping of mules on the trail, was inspired when Grofé was walking past a Los Angeles construction site and heard pile drivers pounding rhythmically.

Americans' inferiority complex and pride helped boost into popularity some quotes from British playwright and novelist J. B. Priestley, who discovered the canyon in the late 1930s. "If I were an American," he wrote, "I should make my remembrance of it the final test of men, art, and politics. I should ask myself: Is this good enough to exist in the same country as the Canyon?"[24]

Priestley became enthralled with the canyon because he was haunted by the mysteries of time, the theme of many of his plays, novels, and metaphysical musings. In the canyon's cliffs Priestley saw the untouchable mystery of time become manifest, and he saw the canyon as part of Einstein's cosmos: "This incredible pageantry of sunlight and chasm, I thought, is our nearest approach to fourth-dimensional scenery. . . . You feel that some element of Time has been conjured into these immensities of Space. Perhaps it is not size nor the huge witchery of changing shapes and shades that fill us with awe, but the obscure feeling that here we have an instantaneous vision of innumerable eons."[25]

This is a more mature vision than the bafflement or debates of the first visitors. Priestley was at home in the scientific cosmos and the aesthetic canyon, but the canyon remained primarily a religious experience: "The Grand Canyon is a sort of landscape Day of Judgment. It is not a show place, a beauty spot, but a revelation. . . . The Colorado River made it, but you feel when you are there that God gave the Colorado River its instructions. It is all Beethoven's nine symphonies in stone and magic light."[26]

In the century since 1919 the Grand Canyon has become a less troubling, more comfortable landscape. This is not just because it has become a familiar image, all over calendars and magazines. Clarence Dutton's challenge that we expand our definitions of natural beauty has been answered so fully that today many people find naked rock to be more real and beautiful than pastoral landscapes. The scientific vision of deep time and strange forces has become more trusted. On the whole, religion has embraced a vaster cosmos. The canyon has lost some power because technological progress has made humans seem more powerful than nature. Technology can also diminish the canyon when visitors experience it through their cameras, not with their hearts.

Yet the Grand Canyon retains its power to draw people out of themselves, to change their sense of reality and possibility, and to let them see that their lives are part of a much greater story.

CHAPTER SEVEN

National Park

If You Build It . . .

When Teddy Roosevelt died in January 1919, ten years after leaving the White House, the Grand Canyon still was not a national park.

Roosevelt had picked William Howard Taft as his successor, but Taft confessed privately that he did not understand Roosevelt's obsession with conservation. Taft visited the Grand Canyon in his first year in office, 1909, but where Roosevelt had delivered an enduring credo of conservation values, Taft's only remembered words were "Golly, what a gully." Taft had been a judge and in 1921 would become the chief justice of the US Supreme Court, and he was much less willing than Roosevelt to stretch the law to serve conservationist passions and began rolling back some of Roosevelt's conservation initiatives.

In the two decades after the Santa Fe Railway arrived and Teddy Roosevelt became president, the Grand Canyon was gathering a stature and a following that became harder to deny. The Santa Fe was promoting the canyon and bringing in growing numbers of tourists; in 1915, as easterners attended the San Francisco World's Fair (which included a six-acre diorama of the Grand Canyon), canyon visitation spiked to one hundred thousand. Arizonans began realizing that tourism might be good business and some businessmen began supporting the creation of a national park, but tourism remained a small part of a state economy increasingly dominated by the mining industry.

Mining might have fizzled out at the Grand Canyon, but massive copper discoveries in southern Arizona had made Arizona the nation's leading copper producer. Mining employed one in five Arizona men and, in 1918, accounted for 58 percent of Arizona's tax revenues. In 1916 Phelps Dodge, Arizona's leading copper company, made twenty-four million dollars in profits, twenty-four times what the Santa Fe Railway had invested to build tracks and facilities for Grand Canyon tourism over nearly two decades. This gave the mining industry enormous political clout. And Phelps Dodge held an old grudge against the Santa Fe Railway. When Phelps Dodge was starting out in the 1880s, it was dependent on the Santa Fe to haul its ores and bring in supplies, and, as usual, the Santa Fe had sucked maximum profits out of Phelps Dodge. When the Santa Fe imperiously refused to build a line to Phelps Dodge's Copper Queen Mine, Phelps Dodge began building its own railroad, a thousand miles of tracks, and tried its best to lure customers away from the Santa Fe. The two railways remained rivals. The power of Phelps Dodge and other mining companies generated a political culture that was hostile to the prospect of the Santa Fe Railway and the federal government ganging up to seize mining claims—even worthless claims inside the Grand Canyon—and other private lands. Ranchers and loggers also bore old grudges against the Santa Fe. The sins of the Santa Fe Railway were coming home to haunt national park advocates.

As the numbers of tourists at the canyon grew, so did the chaos there. No one was planning the growth of the town along the rim. The two roads that arrived from the outside world fizzled out into a maze of muddy tracks. Many employees lived in randomly placed shacks, tents, and boxcars, with stinky outhouses. They were cutting trees for firewood, piling up garbage in plain view, and letting horses graze anywhere. An incinerator near El Tovar Hotel poured out smoke. Because the Santa Fe expected its tourists to stay in its hotels, it did not build a campground, and at first neither did the Forest Service, so the increasing numbers of people showing up by car were camping randomly along roads or in the woods, starting fires and dumping garbage and human waste. At a time when Americans still distrusted the automobile, the Forest Service imposed rules requiring drivers to honk horns when rounding a curve, cresting a hill, or passing a pedestrian or horse from behind, so rim roads were a madhouse of honking horns. The Santa Fe did not want automotive tourists, so it was not building roads for cars, only for buggies for its own passengers. To accommodate the growing need for horses and buggies, the Forest Service opened the door to every liveryman who wanted to come. Too many came, and too many were rough cowboys who treated their competition with rough tactics. Ralph Cameron ran a corral right on the rim, and his cowboys were shoveling horse manure straight into the canyon. Cameron had a "geologist" at a souvenir booth selling bottles of fake Grand Canyon sand, which actually came from elsewhere and was artificially colored. Because the Santa Fe would not allow Cameron's agents on its property, they were standing as close as possible and screaming through megaphones to find customers for Cameron's Hotel, trail rides, or car tours. The Forest Service had long been seduced by the Santa Fe's big money (and better taste) for developing tourist facilities, so it was helping the Santa Fe squeeze out the small operators, even canyon pioneers, causing strong resentments. The Santa Fe finally got fed up with the chaos and declared that it would not spend any more money on tourist facilities until the federal government came up with a better system for running the monument.

In response, in 1916 the Forest Service drew up a plan for reorganizing and developing Grand Canyon Village. When the National Park Service inherited the monument, it retained this plan's basic ideas, making Grand Canyon one of the few national parks with much of a plan for growth—and growth that showed some respect for natural values. The plan's coauthor was twenty-nine-year-old forester Aldo Leopold, who would become one of the pioneers of ecology and a beloved nature writer. In a section titled "What Visitors Are Subjected To," Leopold and his coauthor, Don Johnston, critiqued the "offensive sights and sounds, such as electric advertising signs, megaphone soliciting, etc."[1]

Leopold was appalled by the thriving sport of rolling boulders into the canyon, which the Santa Fe had encouraged in their canyon publicity pamphlet: "Roll a heavy stone to the rim and let it go. It falls sheer the height of a church or an Eiffel Tower ... and explodes like a bomb on a projecting ledge. If, happily, any considerable fragments remain, they bound outward like elastic balls, leaping in a wild parabola from point to point, snapping trees like straws. ... [T]hen there comes languidly up the cliff sides a faint, distant roar, and your bowlder [sic] that had withstood the buffets of centuries lies scattered."[2] Today, the areas most frequented by Santa Fe Railway tourists hold few rim-side boulders.

Leopold and Johnston proposed stopping such abuses and removing much of the clutter from the immediate rim and making it, where still possible, a more natural landscape. They proposed establishing several zones for different types of activities—hotels, support facilities, stables, residences, campgrounds, and commercial stores—with the less essential services hidden from tourists. They admired the buildings of Santa Fe Railway architect Mary Colter, but "most other structures are objectionable in various degrees and ways." When the "objectionable" businesses realized what Leopold and Johnston were planning, they objected strenuously: "One old livery operator," wrote Leopold about his return visit to the canyon in 1917, "stormed at us all morning, which was not so bad, but this afternoon he brought out a frail worn-out wife and four children to do the tear act, which was worse. There is no getting away from the fact that the 'public interest' is sometimes cruel to individuals."[3]

The Forest Service brought in a master landscape planner, Frank Waugh, who turned Leopold and Johnston's recommendations into blueprints for a highly landscaped village with a town square and parkways. These plans were never implemented, but the zones of today's Grand Canyon Village are an imprint of Aldo Leopold's brain. Privately, Waugh held more grandiose plans for developing the canyon, as Leopold wrote, "on a huge scale—a dozen hotels—thousands of cottages—a tramway to the bottom. . . . He is opposed to making a National Park since the Park Service is no good, he says."[4]

At about this same time, Secretary of the Interior Franklin Lane got a letter from an old college classmate, Stephen Mather, who was upset about how the national parks were being mismanaged—or threatened by mining corporations. Secretary Lane replied, "Dear Steve, If you don't like the way the national parks are being run, come on down to Washington and run them yourself."[5] Mather came on down, and he brought great personal energy to the job, although it could be the manic energy of a manic-depressive. His first major task was to push for the creation of a National Park Service, accomplished in 1916. Mather became its first director. Mather's young protégé Horace Albright became assistant director and later Mather's successor, and their nearly two decades of leadership defined much of what people expect to find in national parks today.

Stephen Mather knew all about mining corporations, for he was the president of one. As a young man he had launched his career by coming up with the image and slogan of the "Twenty-Mule Team" for selling Death Valley borax soap, one of the iconic advertising campaigns of the twentieth century. Mather fully understood the mystique of the Wild West. He went on to run his own successful borax mining company, which let him see all the tricks other mining companies pulled to oppose and raid public lands. But Mather had also grown up hiking in the Sierra. Like John Muir, he regarded nature as not only a refuge for the human spirit (including Mather's own spirit when he was depressed) but something spiritual. In his combined love of the Wild West and wild nature, Mather was a lot like Teddy Roosevelt. When American progress finally forced Mather to choose between the two, he chose wilderness. Mather had met and had a long talk with John Muir, and Muir had filled Mather with indignation at the spoiling of the Sierra Nevada. Yet the conservation movement now required more than just indignation and inspiration; it needed a skilled manager. It required more than just advocacy groups like the Sierra Club; it needed a government agency that would develop congressional support for national parks, fight off powerful exploitative interests, and make the parks attractive places for visitors.

With the same salesmanship and sense of American mythos he had used to sell Death Valley soap, Stephen Mather now started promoting Death Valley itself and dozens of other landscapes, including the Grand Canyon. Mather could be very charming and persuasive to politicians and businessmen. Mather thought it disgraceful that the Grand Canyon was still not a national park, and he made this his top priority.

During the Taft and Wilson presidencies, a few congressmen proposed making the canyon a park, but even with the support of the president, the proposals died. One of those proposals would have named it "Andrew Carnegie National Park," in honor of the still living steel tycoon. The US Geological Survey favored the name "Powell National Park," in honor of the late John Wesley Powell. Such suggestions raised the central question that Stephen Mather would need to answer: what is a national park all about? President Roosevelt had helped create two national parks, one in North Dakota and one in Oklahoma, that Mather and his successors decided did not deserve to be national parks, and these parks were demoted into a national wildlife refuge and a national recreation area, respectively. Mather defined national parks as landscapes with a special grandeur and national appeal. And parks should honor nature, not people. Mather did not want the national parks to look like every town square in America, jammed with statues to politicians and generals, so he barred all such memorials inside national parks. Even when friends of the late John Muir asked Mather to approve a plaque honoring Muir in Yosemite, Mather refused. Mather set many high standards for the parks, including architecture, museums, trails, campgrounds, and interpretive programs, standards that have endured until today and made America's national parks admired and

FIGURE 7.1. Stephen Mather, first director of the National Park Service, at Powell Memorial on the canyon rim, built before the park was established.

copied throughout the world. Today a large portion of visitors to western national parks are foreigners, and even those who disapprove of the United States for political or cultural reasons greatly admire the national parks.

Of course, the NPS remains a human institution, subject to trends and compromises. Thus, at today's Grand Canyon you can find a Mather memorial plaque at Mather Point, and there are several other things named for Stephen Mather, including a shopping center, built around 1960. The shopping center's name was appropriate, for Mather had committed the NPS to a philosophy of building services for tourists. Only after a half century, when the parks were "being loved to death," did the NPS begin rethinking its original priorities.

Sometimes compromises were necessary to create new national parks. One of Mather's standards was that he would not allow private lands or resource extraction inside park boundaries. But Mather was also a political realist, and he understood the legal force of the old mining laws. He worked with Arizona's Senator Ashurst and Congressman Hayden to craft a park bill they could accept. While some park advocates wanted to include the forests many miles back from the South Rim, the Ashurst-Hayden bill cut the park boundary very close to the rim, leaving the forests to the loggers and grazers and leaving the rim ecologically illogical as wildlife habitat; in places the boundary was so close to the rim that the NPS could not build a road. The bill protected valid private landholdings inside the park boundaries, though Mather regarded this as a temporary expediency and remained determined to aggressively root out private lands after the park bill passed. The park included just over 1,000 square miles, down quite a bit from the monument's 1,279 square miles. One of the most powerful opponents of park creation was William Randolph Hearst, who feared that a national park would take away the 200 acres he owned at Grandview, so Mather reluctantly agreed not to touch Hearst's land.

The park bill took a year and a half to wind its way through Congress, with private interests pecking at it, but finally it passed. President Woodrow Wilson was in Europe organizing the League of Nations, so the Grand Canyon bill sat on his desk until the day after he returned. Grand Canyon National Park, the League of Nations, and the other big innovation of 1919, Prohibition, flowed from the same well of American moral idealism; only the park would endure. Wilson signed the park bill on February 26, 1919. This was seven weeks after Teddy Roosevelt had died; Roosevelt's admirers considered the park to be a good tribute to him.

The congressional bill that established the National Park Service in 1916 gave it two primary goals. One was to "leave it as it is," to protect natural wonders; the other was to make them accessible for public enjoyment. A bias toward the latter was contained in the word *park*, which implies not a wilderness but a public, pleasantly groomed recreational space. Indeed, Frederick Law Olmsted, the designer of New York City's Central Park, was one of the commissioners of Yosemite, which became a California park in 1864, and his son Frederick Jr. was one of the primary drafters of the NPS's charter. The national parks idea gained a lot of momentum from the parks movement in cities, where parks were prescribed as a cure for the physical and social ills of overcrowded slums. In Central Park the kids of the rich and poor played side by side, and this democratic model affixed itself to national parks, making the American public more willing to evict private interests to create public parks.

At first it was not obvious that the NPS's charter goals of preservation and recreation were contradictory. When 44,000 people arrived at Grand Canyon National Park in its first year, this was an average of 120 people per day, on one daily train, and their main activity was going for long walks along the rim, so they did little damage to nature. But within seventy-five years, 4.5 million people were arriving at the canyon, one hundred times the visitation of 1919, and almost all of them were driving cars or recreational vehicles (RVs), and they expected to find parking places, gas, food, lodging, souvenir shops, and fast highways. From its start the NPS has struggled to balance these two goals. This struggle has led to many compromises, some of which were doomed to fail. Many of the frustrations tourists experience in today's national parks are symptoms of this philosophical dilemma. The NPS does not like seeing drivers unable to find parking places at rim overlooks, but it also does not like bulldozing forests and paving miles of the rim. Hikers and river runners dislike the limited number of permits for inner-canyon adventures, but they also dislike camping in crowds or in spots ruined by overuse. Stephen Mather may have been a visionary, but he never envisioned 4.5 million visitors cramming the Grand Canyon.

Mather did grapple with the NPS's central philosophical dilemma, but he mainly saw the need to build a political constituency for the national parks and accepted Muir's attitude toward tourism and the railroads. The railroads might be motivated by profit and Mather by politics, but the railroads made powerful allies. Mather desperately needed allies. In its first year, the NPS had only $19,500 for its entire Washington, DC, staff. In its first year, Grand Canyon National Park had a budget of only $40,000; that same year, Americans spent $800 million on movie tickets. Mather did not mind if the railroad's park lodges were luxury lodges for the affluent, since the affluent—newspaper publishers, business leaders, politicians, college professors—were the nation's opinion molders. At Grand Canyon Mather continued the Forest Service's practice of favoring the Santa Fe Railway over small operators, and he applied this bias for big business throughout the park system. The salesman in Mather appreciated the effective job the railroads were doing at creating a positive image for the parks. These years gave birth to the modern advertising industry, which used national campaigns to turn obscure products such as Coca-Cola, Wrigley's gum, and Kodak cameras into mass necessities. Western vacations too were advertised as necessities, and most tourists showed up with Kodaks, but for many people a Grand Canyon vacation was an escape from the increasingly loud and phony world of advertising and consumerism, an escape to the real world.

Mather's eagerness to please park visitors gave priority to recreational pleasures. In the 1920s the streams in many national parks were stocked with sport fish, easy enough in a broad valley like Yosemite, but at the Grand Canyon it became truly extravagant. The only perennial streams were in the canyon bottom, so trout were carried down in metal canisters on the backs of mules, even to very remote streams that rarely saw visitors. Four decades later, when Glen Canyon Dam changed the Colorado River into a clear cold-water river, the trout emerged from their side streams, joined trout being stocked into the river, and took over the river—great for fishermen, but a big failure at preserving ecosystems. In other national parks the temptation to please the public led to mere entertainment spectacles, such as Yellowstone's bear feedings and Yosemite's firefall.

The canyon's North Rim was too remote for the Santa Fe Railway, but it did interest the Union Pacific Railroad, which had put its tracks through southwestern Utah and was developing tourism at Zion and Bryce Canyon. Southwestern Utah's ruggedness prevented building tracks to Zion and Bryce Canyon, so the Union Pacific was running bus tours from its nearest stop. The North Rim of the Grand Canyon was quite a bit farther away, through additional rugged landscapes with awful roads, and it was snowbound in winter, so the Union Pacific was cautious about spending much money on tourism there. It started by sending in Thomas and Elizabeth McKee in 1917 to set up a camp of tent cabins, which had wooden floors and frames but canvas tops. Elizabeth McKee was the daughter of William Wylie, who had set up one of the first tourist camps in Yellowstone National Park and was now running a similar camp at Zion. Elizabeth had studied astronomy at Wellesley College and sought a career as an astronomer, but she was rejected merely because she was a woman. The McKees ran their camp for ten years, with a bit of help from a wild burro they befriended, Brighty, who a few decades later became the star of Marguerite Henry's children's novel *Brighty of the Grand Canyon*. When the Union Pacific became convinced that the North Rim would be a popular tourist attraction, it discarded the McKees, demolished their camp, and built an attractive lodge in its place.

The lodge was designed by architect Gilbert Stanley Underwood, who had also designed the Union Pacific's lodges at Zion and Bryce Canyon. For the first of these three lodges, in the heart of Zion Canyon, Underwood had planned a giant building, three stories tall, with two long wings. But Stephen Mather did have his own vision for the parks and was setting some limits to development. Mather overruled Underwood's design, feeling it was so large it would compete against the scenery, and insisted on a less intrusive design. A central building would hold a lobby, restaurant, auditorium for ranger programs, gift shop, and generous observation porches and windows, but all the lodging would be in scattered cabins. This is the design found today at Zion, Bryce Canyon, and the North Rim.

Mather saw that Americans were falling in love with cars, and he encouraged automotive tourism. But no one imagined how fast the automobile would come to dominate American life. In 1908, the year the Grand Canyon became a national monument, Ford introduced the Model T but sold only 309 of them. In 1919, when the canyon became a national park, Ford produced 635,000 Model Ts.

Ironically, the first car trip to the Grand Canyon was sponsored by the Santa Fe Railway to generate publicity for its train business. In January 1902, a few months after the first train arrived at the canyon, the Santa Fe enlisted the editor of the *Los Angeles Herald,* Winfield Hogaboom, and its own photographer Oliver Lippincott to drive from Flagstaff to the canyon in Lippincott's steam-powered, eight-horsepower Toledo Locomobile. Not far out of Flagstaff, the car broke down, the first of several breakdowns. Three days later they were still far from the rim and out of gas, food, and water. They had to walk to Grandview to get help. Pete Berry and his mule team towed the car the rest of the way to the canyon. In 1909 the first two cars arrived at the North Rim, taking three days from Kanab, Utah, nine worn-out tires, and some shovel work.

The Santa Fe's arrival at the South Rim only led to the neglect and deterioration of the roads into the park, already poor. Motorists who attempted the now abandoned stagecoach road from Flagstaff to Grandview got lost and stuck in a maze of deeply rutted ranch roads. The dirt road from Williams was not quite as bad, but it would not become a paved highway until the early 1930s. The roads connecting the South and North Rims were torturous and required crossing the Colorado River on a rickety wooden ferry at Lees Ferry, replaced by Navajo Bridge only in 1929. The road from Kanab to the North Rim benefited from its need to serve Union Pacific tour vehicles, but it also benefited Kanab tire and tow-truck businesses.

Many roads to other national parks were also terrible. The NPS did not have any control over roads outside the parks, so Mather and Albright worked with federal, state, and county agencies, telling them, "If you build it, they will come." In 1920 Coconino County built a decent dirt road (from a point midway between Flagstaff and Williams) to the South Rim. And they did come. In 1920 only 16 percent of canyon visitors came by car, but in 1926 it was more than 50 percent, more than seventy thousand people.

The influx of cars put a lot of pressure on roads inside the park, many of which were also in poor condition. The only paved road in the park was the Santa Fe–built road along the rim to Hermit's Rest. The thirty-two-mile road from Grand Canyon Village to Desert View remained a narrow, bumpy dirt road—when it was not a swamp. The roads to North Rim over-looks were mostly old cattlemen wagon tracks. In its first eight years the NPS built a total of only twelve miles of paved roads in all its parks, due to lack of funds. In 1923 Horace Albright took the US House Appropriations Committee on a tour of the South Rim, and after their cars got stuck in the mud they voted $7.5 million for building roads throughout the parks. Mather began an ambitious road-building program. Some were extraor-dinary engineering feats, such as the Zion–Mt. Carmel Highway in Zion National Park, which cost $1.9 million in 1928 and was justified as a short-cut to the Grand Canyon. Yet through today's more environmentally con-scious eyes, this highway looks like a giant scar on the landscape.

It was symbolic of early NPS priorities that an engineer, Miner Tillot-son, became Grand Canyon National Park's first long-term and important superintendent (1927–38). Many of Mather's park superintendents were engineers. Like the rest of America, the NPS believed in Progress, if in its own way, and Miner Tillotson was a builder. Grand Canyon required more building than other parks, for it was not only busier but more isolated. At other parks employees could live in nearby towns or go there for shopping, medical care, school, or church, but Grand Canyon needed to be a self-contained community; today Grand Canyon is the only national park with its own school—kindergarten through high school.

Born in Indiana, Miner Tillotson studied civil engineering at Purdue and went to work as a construction engineer in San Francisco. When Tillotson's son developed a serious respiratory problem, their doctor recommended moving to a drier climate. Tillotson arrived at the Grand Canyon in 1922 and took charge of building the new park's basic infrastructure, not just

FIGURE 7.2. Miner Tillotson, park superintendent from 1927 to 1938, built much of the park's infrastructure. But all his engineering skills could not stop lightning from knocking a tree onto his car.

roads but scenic overlooks, trails, campgrounds, picnic spots, entrance stations, water systems, ranger offices, and homes. One of his proudest achievements was the rim-to-rim Kaibab Trail and its suspension bridge across the Colorado River, built in 1925–28. But the trail was also a symptom of the political troubles that continued to plague the park.

The NPS renewed the Santa Fe's battle to wrest the Bright Angel Trail away from Ralph Cameron. When Teddy Roosevelt had made the Grand Canyon a national monument, Cameron denounced his action as illegal, and Cameron continued fighting the creation of a national park. In 1920 the US Supreme Court ruled that Cameron's mining claims were bogus and ordered him to vacate his land, but he refused. Instead, he ran for the US Senate as a martyred pioneer, and he promised Arizonans that his Grand Canyon hydroelectric dam would bring cheap electricity for all. Cameron won. Now he had a lot more power for fighting the park. In 1922 Cameron got all appropriations for Grand Canyon National Park removed from the federal budget, at least temporarily. He launched harsh personal attacks against Stephen Mather and tried to get him removed from office. Cameron controlled the park post office, located in his hotel, and his agents intercepted and read NPS mail, forcing rangers to use a secret code to communicate with Mather and Albright in Washington, DC. The NPS offered a deal to Coconino County, which owned Bright Angel Trail, to trade the trail for a modern paved highway the NPS would build from Williams to the canyon, but Cameron rallied county voters to reject the deal. In 1924 the NPS finally gave up trying to obtain the Bright Angel Trail and decided to build its own trail—the South Kaibab—a few miles away.

Unlike other canyon trails, which followed side canyons long used by animals and Native Americans, most of the South Kaibab Trail was blasted out of sheer cliffs. This made it the shortest and steepest trail, six miles to the river. Crossing the river had always been a problem, not solved by a 1907 one-mule cable trolley and a 1921 bridge that swayed alarmingly beneath two steel cables and barely survived a 1923 windstorm. Tillotson built a sturdy, rigid suspension bridge 440 feet (134 m) long, supported by eight steel cables, with a tunnel for an easier approach. The cables weighed 2,030 pounds (913 kg) each, far too much to haul down on mules, so they were carried on the shoulders of about fifty Havasupai, snaking down the trail. The trail to the North Rim was also improved. Tillotson was also engineering a political feat, for as soon as the South Kaibab Trail was completed, tourists would no longer pay a toll for the Bright Angel Trail when they could go down the park trail for free. Coconino County was now less swayed by Ralph Cameron, who had lost his reelection bid in 1926, so the county decided to turn over its trail to the NPS. Now the park had two trails, side by side, to the same place. Now that the Santa Fe Railway had free access to Phantom Ranch and had a bridge that would not terrify the mules, it abandoned its more primitive Hermit Camp and its Hermit Trail.

Trying to define NPS philosophy, Mather and Albright were setting some limits to construction and human impacts in parks. Automobile enthusiasts were pushing for a highway across the heart of the canyon. "To break the age-long silence of the Canyon with the honking of car horns . . . ," wrote Superintendent Tillotson in 1929, "would be sacrilegious indeed." Yet a few sentences later the builder in Tillotson confessed his thrill at the idea: "A bridge to defy the turbulent Colorado! Cliffs that have defied both man and beast, to be conquered by compressed air, powder, and steam shovels! A brand new problem at every turn, and thousands of turns in the road!

What engineer wouldn't give his eye-teeth to be in charge of that job."[6] Mather and Albright said no. Tillotson worked to discourage billboards on the highways approaching the park. They also ruled out a tramway into the canyon or a scenic railroad along the rim. Remembering Hetch Hetchy, Mather and Albright opposed dams and reservoirs inside national parks. They strongly opposed the idea of air tours over national parks, which would shatter the peace and frighten the wildlife. One summer when Albright was serving as superintendent at Yellowstone and a pilot began flying tours over the park and landing in a meadow there, Albright raced out, confronted him, and threatened to personally seize his plane if he ever returned. Opposing air tours took political guts, for the man trying to set up an air-tour company covering many national parks was a cousin of Teddy Roosevelt and the brother of Eleanor Roosevelt, soon to be first lady.

In 1932 President Herbert Hoover created a new Grand Canyon National Monument, holding 426 square miles to the west of the national park, including the Toroweap Valley with its extinct volcanoes and lava flows cascading into the Colorado River. The new monument was managed by the national park, though its remoteness meant it received little visitation or development. In 1975 the monument would be absorbed into the national park.

The Great Depression brought declining visitation and budgets to Grand Canyon National Park. Visitation dropped from 188,204 in 1929 to 108,823 in 1933. But the Depression also turned into a bonanza for the national parks. Teddy Roosevelt's lingering image as a daring man of action helped get his cousin Franklin elected president in 1932; Franklin had modeled himself on Teddy, including a love for conservation. As a legislative man of action, Franklin Roosevelt quickly created the Civilian Conservation Corps, which poured a great deal of manpower and money into the national parks and other lands. The CCC was justified as a jobs program; over nine years it employed more than 3 million young men and supported their destitute families back home. They planted more than 3 *billion* trees and built 28,088 miles of trails and 52,320 acres of public campgrounds.

Less than three months after Franklin Roosevelt's inauguration, the CCC arrived at the Grand Canyon. They set up camps on both rims and at Phantom Ranch at the canyon bottom, with as many as 797 CCC boys working at one time. They carried out many of the projects on Miner Tillotson's agenda. They built new inner-canyon trails and improved older trails. They

FIGURE 7.3. The Civilian Conservation Corps carving the River Trail out of sheer cliffs, ca. 1935.

built hundreds of miles of boundary fences to finally stop cattle from invading the park. They built a telephone line across the canyon, campgrounds, picnic shelters, roads, park buildings, houses, waterworks, a fire lookout, rim walkways, and a lot more. Most of their work has endured well.

Franklin Roosevelt's secretary of the interior, Harold Ickes, had gotten into politics because he was inspired by Teddy Roosevelt. Ickes felt that Mather and Albright had led the NPS too far from Teddy's "leave it as it is" values. Like Teddy, Ickes hated having railroad-built luxury hotels in national parks, when parks should be thoroughly democratic. Ickes regretted Mather's road-building campaign and held that national parks should not be for cars but for people to go hiking and horseback riding. This was a bold position, considering that Ickes's boss, Franklin Roosevelt, paralyzed by polio, could not walk anywhere and did all of his park touring by car. Ickes was the first secretary of the interior to hold that wilderness should be preserved for its own sake, not just for human use. Ickes was both three decades too late and three decades ahead of his time. He hardly deflected the NPS's "build-it" momentum. But Ickes did succeed, through a condemnation suit, in taking over William Randolph Hearst's Grandview lands.

A growing NPS success story was the public programs offered by ranger-naturalists, many of whom had science backgrounds and did scientific research in their free time. At the canyon this role was lastingly defined by Eddie McKee (no relation to Thomas and Elizabeth McKee), who started in 1929 and remained at the park for eleven years. These were almost the same years that Miner Tillotson was building the park's infrastructure, and McKee built its intellectual infrastructure, its public programs and museums. McKee had a geology degree from Cornell, but his curiosity was wide and deep, and so was his capacity for rugged treks. Much of the natural history of the Grand Canyon had barely been explored, so for McKee it was a research paradise and he made many pioneering discoveries and collections.

One time when McKee was hiking out of the canyon, he spotted a pink rattlesnake that he recognized was an unknown species. He had to have it, but he did not have any sack for holding a snake. He grabbed the snake around the neck and carried it out of the canyon to his car. But his car had no container for a snake, so he held the snake out the window with one hand while he drove with the other hand. One summer he met a young lady biologist, Barbara, doing research on the North Rim, and Eddie would hike fifty round-trip miles (eighty kilometers) across the canyon to visit her. Barbara was impressed, and soon she was Barbara McKee.

In 1937 Eddie McKee and Miner Tillotson went on a scientific expedition to Shiva Temple, a sheer-cliffed mesa inside the canyon, long separated from the canyon rim. A scientist from the American Museum of Natural History, Harold E. Anthony, theorized that in the isolation atop Shiva Temple some animals might have evolved into unique species. He was thinking of insects or mice. But when newspaper reporters heard about the expedition, they imagined that Shiva Temple might be a "lost world" full of dinosaurs, and they gave the expedition major publicity. South Rim photographer Emery Kolb thought the whole thing was ridiculous and that Shiva Temple could not be all that hard to reach, so he sneaked up it ahead of the expedition and left some Kodak film canisters on the ground as his calling card. The scientists found some ancient pottery sherds and no special biology.

FIGURE 7.4. Park ranger Eddie McKee and his biologist wife,
Barbara, at the top of Tanner Trail, 1931.

Miner Tillotson's successor as superintendent, Harold C. Bryant, who
would serve for fourteen years, had a biology PhD from the University of
California at Berkeley and had done important research in animal behav-
ior and ecosystems; in his twenties he was writing papers such as "Noctur-
nal Wanderings of the California Pocket Gopher." In 1919 Bryant was giving a public talk at Lake Tahoe when a vacationing Stephen Mather saw
him, was very impressed, and recruited Bryant to give public programs at

Yosemite. Soon Bryant took charge of developing interpretative programs for the entire national park system. When Bryant became superintendent at Grand Canyon, he declared that his arrival represented a maturing of NPS values. The era of park "acquisition, protection, and physical development" was yielding to the "educational and appreciation phase," in which canyon visitors would be imbued "with its natural beauty and charm." Developing nature appreciation was Bryant's main love at Grand Canyon; this included building a large natural history collection for both science and public education. Bryant was ahead of his time in making policy decisions from an ecological perspective. Yet he was also premature in saying that the parks were done with "physical development."

After World War II growing national prosperity and pent-up demand for travel brought a surge in visitation to the Grand Canyon: 622,363 people in 1947, more than 1 million in 1956. The rise of interstate highways, air travel, and rental-car companies meant that reaching the Grand Canyon was easier, including from overseas; foreign visitors would make up as much as 40 percent of the total. Park facilities built for much smaller numbers were being overwhelmed. Many buildings were now decades old and decaying. Railroad tourism was dying out fast—the Santa Fe discontinued passenger service to the canyon in 1966—and old park roads were crumbling under the new demands of cars.

In 1956 the NPS launched a major national construction program called Mission 66, aimed at greatly expanding park facilities by the fiftieth anniversary of the NPS in 1966. Nationwide, it would spend about $1 billion and build or rebuild 100 visitor centers, 575 campgrounds, 1,197 miles (1,925 km) of roads, 1,502 parking lots, and much more. It also called upon private concessionaires to greatly expand park lodging and restaurants.

Mission 66 made Grand Canyon National Park one of its highest priorities. In 1957 the park got the first of the 100 new visitor centers, costing nearly $500,000. Park planners decided not to try to pack the new buildings into Grand Canyon Village, which had been built around the old Santa Fe Railway station. Instead, they built a new complex of buildings a mile to the east, closer to where cars first entered the park.

Near the new Visitor Center was an outdoor amphitheater for ranger programs and the Shrine of the Ages for wintertime ranger programs and for church services and community activities. Across the street was the "Mather Business Zone," with a grocery store, bank, post office, gas station,

FIGURE 7.5. Tourist at south entrance station, 1931. By 1926, with encouragement from the NPS, park visitation by car had surpassed visitation by train.

cafeteria, souvenir shop, and Yavapai Lodge. Nearby was the Mather Campground and another area for trailers. Visitor services were also expanded at Desert View and in Grand Canyon Village. Mission 66 also expanded park staffing, and this required much more housing. Yet park visitation continued expanding faster than planners had imagined. Nationwide, national park visitation rose from 61 million in 1956 to 133 million in 1966. After all the money and all the construction, visitor services were still being overwhelmed.

The expanding services on the South Rim were fast approaching a major barrier, a shortage of water. The rim had no source of fresh water, and as for wells, the water table lay 3,000 feet down through solid rock. For the first thirty years, daily Santa Fe tanker cars brought in all the water used on the South Rim. This prompted the NPS to develop a pioneering water reclamation system. But by the late 1920s the South Rim was facing a water crisis. The Santa Fe decided to follow the example of the Union

Pacific, which in 1927–29 had solved the North Rim's water issues by building a pipeline 3,000 vertical feet down to an abundant inner-canyon spring, Roaring Springs. In 1930–32 the Santa Fe built a pipeline to Indian Garden, a less roaring spring halfway down the Bright Angel Trail. But even then the Santa Fe had to haul in additional water in peak seasons for another three decades. The Mission 66 building projects, plus the coming demise of the trains, forced the NPS to come up with a new solution: a pipeline that ran from the South Rim to the canyon bottom, crossed the river on a new bridge, and snaked underneath the North Kaibab Trail for ten miles to an improved pump house at Roaring Springs.

It was one of the most ambitious engineering feats in park history, and it was nearly finished in December 1966. Then the heaviest storm in park history dumped two years' worth of rain into Bright Angel Creek and Crystal Creek within two days. The flood down Crystal Creek ripped out Ancestral Puebloan ruins that had been there for nearly a thousand years and transformed the rocky but manageable Crystal Rapid into one of the most feared rapids in America. The flood down Bright Angel Creek ripped the new pipeline to shreds. In another era, to the ancient Greeks or Native Americans, the flood might have been taken as punishment for human hubris, for humans imagining they could conquer nature. In 1966 it was merely a temporary setback.

But the word *hubris* was occurring to quite a few people over another Grand Canyon water project under way at this same time. Hoover Dam had already flooded dozens of miles of the lower Grand Canyon, and now the Bureau of Reclamation was planning two more dams within the canyon itself. Marble Canyon Dam would flood the canyon's first 40 miles (64 km) and permanently end river running. Bridge Canyon Dam would flood 95 miles (152 km) of the lower river, including its most famous rapid, Lava Falls, and its most famous side canyon, Havasu Canyon. Now, two-thirds of the Grand Canyon would be flooded. In one proposal what remained of the Colorado River would be diverted through a 54-mile (86-km) tunnel to another side canyon, Kanab Creek, where it would power another hydroelectric plant. All this electricity would be used to pump Colorado River water hundreds of miles, over mountains and across deserts, for the sake of golf courses and swimming pools in Phoenix.

Leaders of Grand Canyon National Park and NPS director Conrad Wirth opposed the dams, but Secretary of the Interior Stewart Udall told them to keep quiet. This was ironic, for Wirth was the mastermind of Mission 66 and Udall did not like all the construction going on in the parks. Yet Udall was also an Arizonan—a great-grandson of John D. Lee, of Lees Ferry—and loyal to a culture in which maximizing water resources remained a strong commandment. Into this leadership void stepped the Sierra Club. In an advertising campaign worthy of Stephen Mather, the Sierra Club ran full-page ads in the *New York Times* comparing flooding the Grand Canyon to flooding the Sistine Chapel. Public outrage flooded Congress, which banned the dams. The Grand Canyon dam controversy was a major catalyst in the growth of the conservation movement.

The dams were also important symbols in an ongoing cultural debate about technology, which Americans had always seen as heroic but now were deciding could also be destructive. Amid the Grand Canyon dam debate John Steinbeck wrote *America and Americans,* and in a chapter about the land he wrote: "From early times we were impressed and awed by the fantastic accidents of nature, like the Grand Canyon. . . . But we are an exuberant people, careless and destructive as active children. We make strong and potent toys and then have to use them to prove that they exist. Under the pressure of war we finally made the atom bomb . . . and I think we finally frightened ourselves."[7]

The dam proposals got as far as they did because neither was located inside the national park. For years, park advocates had wanted to expand the park's boundaries to include its whole geological reality, not just the popular tourist areas. On his final day in the White House in 1969, President Lyndon B. Johnson created Marble Canyon National Monument, which gave some protection to the canyon's first 52 miles (83 km) and placed another obstacle against further dam projects. Six years later both it and Grand Canyon National Monument, downstream from the park, were added to the park.

The hubris of human technology at the Grand Canyon in this era also resulted in a human tragedy. In the 1950s the airline business was growing much faster than safety regulations. After taking off from an airport, pilots were free to go their own way. On June 30, 1956, two airliners, carrying a total of 128 people, were following parallel routes from Los Angeles to the Midwest. Both pilots left their plotted course so their passengers could get a good view of the Grand Canyon. One plane was 5 miles (8 km) off course, the other 25 miles (40 km). The two planes were supposed to be flying at different altitudes, 2,000 feet (609 m) apart, but the first pilot rose to the same altitude as the second and no one warned the second pilot. Like cars, planes have blind spots, and the pilots were probably also preoccupied looking at the canyon. North of the Desert View area one plane overtook the other from above and behind, slashing off the tail of the first plane, slashing off its own wing. Both planes plunged into the canyon. One hundred and twenty-eight deaths made this the worst air disaster in US history up to that time. The location of many of the bodies, high atop a butte, required a Swiss mountain-rescue team to reach them. The crash debris, resting atop the fossils of species that had gone extinct because they could not change their ways, remained there for decades, sparkling in the sun, visible to tourists on the rim.

In 1969 park visitation reached 2 million, and in 1976 it hit 3 million. Some of this increase was inspired by the appreciation of nature that was growing through the 1960s. But visitors were having a harder time finding an inspiring experience. Entrance stations, parking lots, and cafeterias were clogged. Parks were full of traffic accidents, crime, and litter. In campgrounds stereos blared music, including lines about how they paved paradise and put up a parking lot. Forests were being bulldozed to build bland motels. The canyon's air was sometimes so polluted that the opposite rim became a blur. Decades of forest mismanagement were generating ever-larger forest fires. The uranium mine on Hermit Road was spewing out dust and noise, and trucks loaded with uranium ore were parading through the park. Planes and helicopters, both sightseeing and private, were roaring overhead anywhere they wanted, sometimes crashing and killing people. Tourists looking into the canyon saw a maze of paths carved by feral burros, and because of the burros, tourists no longer saw native bighorn sheep. Many of the native fish in the Colorado River had been killed off by the much colder water coming from Glen Canyon Dam, and the altered river flows were eroding the beaches needed by wildlife and river runners. Tamarisk trees had marched along the river corridor and crowded out native plants. A thousand people were showing up at Phantom Ranch and trying to camp in a campground designed for 75 people. Rafters were leaving beaches piled with trash, campfire ashes, and human sewage; one time the NPS hauled out three tons of garbage, at its own expense, since river companies were operating without paying any fees.

Clearly, something had gone wrong. Every step of the way had seemed logical enough. The canyon needed to be a national park. Parks needed tourists. Tourists needed food. Cars needed parking lots. But somehow it had all added up wrong. John Muir's philosophy of encouraging tourism had evolved into a circus that would have appalled him.

Through the din of car horns, the ghost of Teddy Roosevelt saying "leave it as it is" was actually becoming easier to hear.

CHAPTER EIGHT

Architecture
Buildings Grown by the Canyon Itself

Artists spent decades trying to figure out how to do justice to the Grand Canyon, but when it came to architecture the canyon was lucky: it soon attracted and helped to inspire a genius, Mary Colter, who had a powerful vision of what the Southwest should look like. She would design eight buildings or complexes of buildings at the canyon, and she helped to define what kind of architecture belonged in other national parks.

The conflict between European habits and southwestern realities is dramatically illustrated by the juxtaposition of two buildings in the center of Grand Canyon Village. Both buildings were built by the Santa Fe Railway, and both opened in January 1905. They are only a hundred feet apart, but in their inspirations they are worlds apart. One is El Tovar Hotel, and the other is Mary Colter's Hopi House.

With El Tovar the Santa Fe Railway was trying to outdo the Northern Pacific Railroad's Old Faithful Inn in Yellowstone. Both hotels were built as destinations that would give people a good reason to take an expensive train trip to the West and to stay in one place for a week or two. The Santa Fe Railway spent a quarter of a million dollars on El Tovar, nearly twice as much as the Northern Pacific had spent on Old Faithful Inn. El Tovar was state of the art, with electric lights, running hot water, steam heat, and a lot of luxuries. It included an art gallery where guests could purchase Thomas Moran's Europeanized visions of the Grand Canyon.

Like Thomas Moran's fake Italian colors, El Tovar was an imposition upon the canyon. Architect Charles F. Whittlesey designed El Tovar as a mixture of Swiss and Nordic styles; tourists who were looking for Arizona found themselves eating in the Norway Dining Room. In these years before World War I, Americans had a lot of enthusiasm for Germanic, Wagnerian imagery, and the Santa Fe advertised El Tovar as a "Rhine Castle," though it included little of the stone suggested by the word *castle*. El Tovar's lobby, meant to invoke a rustic hunting lodge, included the stuffed heads of two moose, though moose could not live in the Grand Canyon's dry climate. El Tovar was built of fir trees brought all the way from Oregon, though nearby ponderosa forests were being used for buildings all over the Southwest. El Tovar was named for Pedro Álvarez de Tovar, a Spanish captain who dispatched the party of Spanish explorers who "discovered" the Grand Canyon, but Tovar himself never saw the canyon. El Tovar Hotel's European persona was intended to answer the long-standing feeling of affluent Americans that touring Europe was more important than touring America; the railroads were urging Americans to "See America First," but they knew that some European-flavored lodgings would help.

El Tovar was one of several hotels that the Santa Fe Railway named for Spanish conquistadores, who had committed many brutalities against Native Americans, including the Hopis. In the Pueblo revolt of 1680, the Hopis threw the Spanish over the cliffs and tore down their missions, built with forced labor. Fearing a return of the Spanish, the Hopis moved some of their villages to the tops of mesas, and they continued an old architectural tradition of placing the entrances to their houses in the roofs, reachable only by retractable ladders. While Whittlesey was building his tribute to the conquistadores, Mary Colter was answering him with a three-story Hopi "castle" shaped to defend the ancient Southwest against European invaders.

When Mary Colter designed Hopi House, America had been entirely conquered by European architecture. The United States was filled with buildings that were Greek, Romanesque, Italianate, Gothic, Renaissance, Georgian, Victorian, Queen Ann, Tudor, and Beaux-Arts. Americans had absorbed virtually nothing from Native American traditions. Americans had decided that if the Southwest had a "look," it was Spanish-mission style, which was indeed designed for a desert climate, but Spanish-mission style was not just European; it also contained large Islamic influences from the long Moorish control of Spain. Spanish missions were descended from medieval fortresses, with their towers, sturdy surrounding walls, gates, and thick church walls; with the Alamo this design served its old purpose and became a star of Texas history, but in Arizona history Spanish missions were much less important and they had no connection at all with the Grand Canyon. When Mary Colter arrived at the canyon and pondered how to do architectural justice to the American land, Frank Lloyd Wright— nearly the same age as Colter—was working on this same question in

Chicago and creating a distinctly American architecture, with shapes that fitted the prairie.

Mary Colter's answer was similar to Wright's. Two of her Grand Canyon buildings, Lookout Studio and Hermit's Rest, were meant to fit into the canyon's shapes and rocks and colors, to emerge seamlessly from the layers of rock beneath them, as if the canyon were dreaming up and growing its own buildings. Two other buildings, Hopi House and the Desert View Watchtower, were inspired by Native American culture, especially by the Hopis, who belonged to the canyon more deeply than anyone else could.

Hopi House was Colter's re-creation of the Hopi dwellings she had seen in the ancient town of Oraibi on the Hopi mesas. She took pains to be accurate in her designs and materials, and she employed Hopi workers to do much of the work. As with all of her Grand Canyon buildings, Colter used local stones so that the buildings would blend in with the geology and local wood with its natural twists. The ceiling of Hopi House was made of logs and layers of interwoven branches and twigs, with the leaves still on them. On the outside, rough ladders reached to the terraced upper floors.

Colter did add conventional ground-floor doorways, but she insisted that the doorways had to be as low as in real pueblos, which meant that American tourists had a high risk of bumping their heads—today the door lintels are stained with blood and flesh oils. Colter's bosses at the Santa Fe Railway and the Fred Harvey Company must have been dismayed at this prospect, but they let Colter have her way, as they usually would. We can suspect that Colter liked the idea that Americans needed to bow their heads in honor of Native Americans.

Hopi House really did serve as a house for Hopis, who lived upstairs and worked on the main floor demonstrating the making of Hopi arts. One of the first demonstrators was Nampeyo, the most famous of all Hopi potters, who restored to Hopi pottery many of its ancient designs. Hopi House was part museum, part demonstration area, and part sales shop offering Native American arts to the tourists staying at El Tovar. Though the Santa Fe and Fred Harvey Company were happy to exploit Native Americans and their culture, they also gave Mary Colter a lot of money and artistic freedom to create accurate tributes to Native American culture. For Colter, this was also a way of honoring the Grand Canyon.

Mary Colter's admiration for Native American culture began with her youth in St. Paul, Minnesota. Colter was born in Pittsburgh in 1869 (a few

FIGURE 8.1. Louis Akin's 1904 painting of El Tovar Hotel and Hopi House (on rim).

weeks before John Wesley Powell launched his expedition down the Colorado River), and her parents moved her to St. Paul in 1880. This was only four years after the Little Big Horn and ten years before Wounded Knee; Plains tribes and cultures were still energetic, and Mary became fascinated by them. She loved some Sioux drawings she had been given. When a smallpox epidemic was devastating the Sioux population and Mary's mother got the idea that she should burn all the Indian items in the house, Mary hid her Sioux drawings to save them.

Mary's hopes of attending art school were threatened by the death of her father when she was seventeen, which left the Colters in precarious financial shape. Mary made a deal with her mother: if Mary could attend an art and design school in San Francisco, she would return to St. Paul and get a teaching job to support the family. In San Francisco Mary also pursued her interest in architecture, apprenticing with an architect. Colter never received any academic training as an architect and never got an architect's license—very few women could at that time. When Colter drew up architectural plans for her buildings, she had to get a licensed Santa Fe Railway architect to sign them for her. Both within the company and in the newspapers, Colter was often called a "decorator," which helped prevent her from getting the recognition she deserved as an architect.

After art school Colter returned to St. Paul and taught drawing at the Mechanic Arts High School for fifteen years. In both San Francisco and St. Paul, Colter absorbed the emerging Arts and Crafts style, a British-born movement that rejected industrialism and favored the rustic. Colter might have remained a schoolteacher for life, but at some point she met Minnie Harvey Huckel, the daughter of Fred Harvey and the wife of John Huckel, who after Fred Harvey's death in 1901 became one of the leaders of the company. Minnie Harvey Huckel loved Native American arts and helped persuade the company to start an Indian Department to gather and sell southwestern arts to tourists. The Fred Harvey Company was planning a grand railroad-trackside hotel for Albuquerque, designed in Spanish-mission style by Charles F. Whittlesey, and it would include an Indian Building for selling Indian arts. The Indian Building too would be done in Spanish-mission style, but no one had much of an idea of what the inside of an Indian shop should look like.

Today we readily recognize certain items and design motifs as quintessentially "southwestern." These items include Navajo rugs and sand paintings, Hopi katsina dolls, Puebloan pottery, turquoise jewelry, and pop-culture motifs such as howling coyotes. Southwestern-style buildings are decorated with designs taken from Navajo rugs and Puebloan pottery and with colors from the land itself. Yet in 1900 relatively few Americans even recognized these items and motifs. No one had thought much about which designs might best represent the Southwest or what items tourists might want to take home to decorate their own homes. For its Indian Building the Fred Harvey Company needed to find a designer with a lot of understanding of Native American arts and a lot of imagination and judgment. It took a chance on Mary Colter. The results so delighted both tourists and company managers that the Fred Harvey Company would employ Colter for nearly a half century. Her next assignment was another hotel–Indian shop pairing with Charles F. Whittlesey, at the Grand Canyon. But this time Colter was given the freedom and resources to design her own building.

The Santa Fe Railway approved and paid for all of Mary Colter's buildings in a remarkable act of vision and artistic patronage. From an architectural world almost entirely dominated by men, they pulled not just a woman but a very feisty and tough woman who was determined to have her artistic visions fulfilled. When construction workers placed a stone in the wrong place, she ordered them to tear down a wall and rebuild it.

The Santa Fe Railway's respect for a strong woman architect may have been encouraged by the fact that the Santa Fe was already famous as an enclave of strong women, the Harvey Girls who staffed its restaurants. Fred Harvey was a dapper Englishman who was appalled by the bad meals and lodgings along America's western railways, and starting in 1876 he began setting up far more reliable and elegant tourist services for the Santa Fe line. For waitresses he recruited young eastern women, often well educated and pretty, who had a taste for adventure and used their jobs to explore the West. In Victorian America the Harvey Girls were the most visible and respected female workforce. Their waitress dresses might be Victorian, but their spirit was more typical of the American frontier. Fred Harvey may have taken a few hints from one of his best friend's sisters, Susan B. Anthony, whose namesake niece, "Susie B.," grew up with Fred Harvey's daughter Minnie (who discovered Mary Colter) and with sons Ford and Byron, who later led the company and supervised Colter. In the late 1800s there was a serious shortage of single women in the West, so the Fred Harvey restaurants attracted a lot of local men, including pioneers who were building major ranches, businesses, and political careers. The Harvey Girls who married these men became the founders of some of the leading families of the West. The loss of Harvey Girls to marriages became so serious that the company added a contract clause that Harvey Girls could not get married for up to one year after starting work. The role of the Harvey Girls in civilizing the West was celebrated in the 1946 MGM musical *The Harvey Girls,* in which Judy Garland sang Johnny Mercer's song "On the Atchison, Topeka, and the Santa Fe." When the movie came out, Mary Colter was still designing buildings for the Santa Fe.

However much Gilded Age railroads viewed national parks in terms of profits, they also deserve credit for sharing the American vision of the national parks as icons of national pride and shrines of natural grandeur. In architecture they could have gotten away with buildings that were far more conventional and less expensive. Yet they sought out visionary young architects and left a dignified legacy for future generations.

The Union Pacific Railroad assigned its North Rim lodge to Gilbert Stanley Underwood, who had just finished building the Ahwahnee Hotel in Yosemite, which many fans of national park architecture consider to be the best lodge in any national park. As with Mary Colter, the railroad hired Underwood when he was in his early thirties and had no professional track record to recommend him; all he had was a vision. Underwood built Grand Canyon Lodge in 1928 out of the limestone that makes up the canyon rim, and he was probably influenced by Mary Colter in trying to make the lodge look like a natural extension of the cliffs. The lodge is visible to the naked eye from the South Rim, but even tourists with binoculars have trouble distinguishing it from the cliffs. For timber Underwood used local ponderosa trees. At his other park lodges, including at Zion and Bryce Canyon, Underwood used local materials and tried to blend the buildings into the landscape. Grand Canyon Lodge burned down in 1932 but was soon rebuilt in the same basic pattern.

Nearly a decade after completing Hopi House, Mary Colter returned to the Grand Canyon and designed her two geological buildings, Hermit's Rest and Lookout Studio, both built in 1914. Hermit's Rest stood at the end of the Santa Fe's new eight-mile West Rim road and at the beginning of its Hermit Trail into the canyon, which reached Hermit Camp deep inside the canyon. All of these "hermit" names referred to prospector Louis Boucher, who may have spent a lot of time alone in the canyon but was not a hermit in spirit; he enjoyed the company of tourists. Mary Colter liked the mythic idea of a canyon hermit, and she designed Hermit's Rest as if it had been built by a rugged prospector as his rocky den, dug into a hillside. Its irregular stones were piled with seeming crudeness, but inside it contained elegant stone arches and a large fireplace. As one of Colter's tricks to make the building look old, she stained the fireplace wall with soot. Colter's tribute to Louis Boucher was a bit ironic, for Boucher felt that the Santa Fe Railway had wrecked his own tourist business and he had left the canyon in 1909. Lookout Studio was perched on the canyon rim not far from El Tovar. It offered an all-season shelter for viewing the canyon, with a large fireplace for staying warm and several observation decks, both inside and outside.

When Aldo Leopold came to the canyon in 1915 to make his development plan, he found Colter's new buildings "exceptionally attractive. As long as the Company's work is passed upon by Miss Colter ... its appropriateness can be assured."[1] In 1917 Leopold took a weeklong trip into the canyon, accompanied by Colter and a few others.

In the early 1930s Colter preferred a similar geological design for a new lodge, the Bright Angel. She wanted a stone building on the rim, blending into it. But now that the Grand Canyon was a national park, the NPS had to approve of new buildings, and it did not want a large building that interrupted the popular rim promenade. Colter set Bright Angel Lodge farther back from the rim and redesigned it as a lower ranch-style log and stone building. In the lounge she celebrated canyon geology by designing a ten-foot-high fireplace made from all the strata of rock inside the canyon.

In 1922 Colter designed Phantom Ranch at the canyon bottom, the destination for overnight journeys on the famous Grand Canyon mules. As at Bright Angel Lodge, its guest cabins were Arts and Crafts style.

Colter's masterpiece was the Desert View Watchtower, opened in 1933 at the eastern entrance to the park. Like Hermit's Rest and Lookout Studio, the Watchtower is perched on the canyon rim and seems to grow naturally out of its cliffs. While the seventy-foot tower offers a great view of the canyon, it is mainly a shrine to Native American culture, especially the Hopis, whose sacred place of emergence is located in the gorge of the Little Colorado River, visible in the distance. Colter was inspired by the towers built by the Ancestral Puebloans in the Four Corners area, particularly Hovenweep. At a time when many of these towers had barely been examined by archaeologists, Colter—now in her early sixties—spent months studying them. She rented an airplane to scout out towers, and then she traveled into some very remote areas to study and sketch the towers and ponder their purpose. She tried to make her Watchtower look authentic and ancient, adding a broken rim, walled-up doors, and an imitation ruin beside the tower.

Inside the Watchtower Hopi artist Fred Kabotie painted murals depicting the meanings the Grand Canyon holds for Hopis. Fred Kabotie's father had helped to lead Hopi resistance against assimilation, and for Fred painting was a way to uphold Hopi traditions. The style of his Watchtower murals was inspired by murals archaeologists had recently discovered in ancient abandoned Hopi kivas. While attending art school in Santa Fe, Fred Kabotie happened to meet Fred Harvey's granddaughter Kitty, who bought some of his artwork. Twenty years after his Watchtower murals, Fred Kabotie painted another mural in the new cocktail lounge in the Bright Angel Lodge, a mural showing fat, lazy white tourists who were failing to appreciate the Grand Canyon. It appears that Fred Kabotie shared the mixed feelings of many Native Americans about tourism.

Other levels in the Watchtower are richly painted with motifs taken from

FIGURE 8.2. Mary Colter (*right*) studying a kiva and tower at Mesa Verde, seeking inspiration and accuracy for her Desert View Watchtower.

ancient rock art. Small windows filter the light into soft, eerie church-like tones, while on the top floor large picture windows offer brilliant views of the canyon. The round entrance room was meant to invoke a kiva, the Puebloans' ceremonial chamber; Colter did not intend it to be the busy gift shop it later became. With the Desert View Watchtower Mary Colter was encouraging respect for Native American culture and proclaiming that the Grand Canyon was a spiritual place, a place for encountering the depths of time and creation.

Mary Colter also designed and decorated a dozen buildings outside of Grand Canyon National Park. She designed two hotels: El Navajo in Gallup, New Mexico, a modernistic concrete building filled with Navajo designs; and La Posada in Winslow, Arizona, an elaborate Spanish hacienda. She decorated La Fonda Hotel in Santa Fe and Union Station in Los Angeles. Yet as railroad travel died out, Mary Colter saw some of her buildings die. In 1957 El Navajo was torn down to widen Route 66, and La Posada was closed. "There's such a thing as living too long," she mourned.[2] She died the next year.

During the years Mary Colter was designing her Grand Canyon buildings, the most famous female architect in America was Julia Morgan, best known for Hearst Castle at San Simeon. William Randolph Hearst directed Morgan to design several buildings for the land he owned on the rim of the Grand Canyon. She designed a home, a hotel, and a museum for Hearst's collection of Native American art. None was ever built. The designs were done in pueblo style and were probably influenced by Mary Colter's buildings.

In these same years the NPS was trying to figure out its own style for park architecture. Like Aldo Leopold, Grand Canyon rangers became great admirers of Colter's buildings. Colter had a large influence on the "National Park Service Rustic" style found throughout the national park system today. This style emphasizes stone and wood and the woodsy colors green and brown. The stonework tries to match the stone of the local landscape, and the wood is left as rough timbers, as in pioneer log cabins, rather than smoothed beams and boards. The NPS adopted this style for its first generation of visitor centers, museums, shelters, amphitheaters, offices, and residences, and in the 1930s the Civilian Conservation Corps built a second generation of buildings in rustic style.

Yet in the 1950s Mission 66 broke from the rustic tradition. Mission 66 was all about Progress, and this included architectural progress. Mission 66 was launched in the heyday of the architectural style called "modernism," which emphasized steel and glass rather than stone and wood, disapproved of forms that did not have functions, and discouraged ornamentation. Modernism discouraged local uniqueness and left buildings all over the world looking exactly alike. Many Mission 66 buildings were quite bland and could have belonged in a big-city downtown or in a suburban shopping center as easily as in a national park. The Mission 66 buildings at Grand Canyon National Park now seem lifeless beside Colter's buildings. By the start of the twenty-first century, the NPS had reembraced the rustic style.

Americans have always been a forward-looking people, eager to embrace the new and replace the old. This may have served Americans well in technology, but in architecture it has led to the destruction of many thousands of beautiful and historically important buildings. Yet perhaps Mary Colter did not live long enough, for within two decades after her death Americans had begun to better appreciate the value of their history. In architecture there can be no deeper history than buildings inspired by two billion years of rocks and millennia of Native American life.

CHAPTER NINE

The Environmental Era

Seeing Nature from the Inside

When Henry David Thoreau started living in his cabin at Walden Pond in 1845, even his nature-loving friends like Emerson thought Henry was rather eccentric. Thoreau's book *Walden* made little impact and remained obscure for decades. Thoreau seemed unqualified to become a patron saint of American environmentalists a century after his death: he never saw the American West, he did not see nature in ecological or evolutionary terms, and he said hardly a word about defending nature against development. Yet in the 1960s *Walden* was being devoured on American college campuses and being stuffed into backpacks for hikes into the Grand Canyon. Thoreau's sainthood revealed a lot about the cultural sources of the swelling interest in nature and conservation. Most of Thoreau's readers had grown up in cities and suburbs in an America that was no longer a nation of poor, striving immigrants but an affluent nation flaunting its status symbols. Yet affluence had only exposed the poverty of American social values, in which material success was all that mattered. A generation of spiritually hungry young people set out to find something more nourishing, and they found Thoreau saying that human society and material success were not so important and that nature was a more meaningful reality.

Atop this cultural undercurrent were the more obvious physical symptoms of something gone wrong: air and water pollution, toxic wastes, oil spills, and chemical poisons bringing silent springs to suburban backyards. At the same time, ecological ideas had grown into an authoritative science. From these various sources major new energy flowed into the conservation movement and transformed it into a powerful cultural force and a political mass movement. It also took a new name: environmentalism. Whereas the name *conservation* tended to mean saving some special places and species, *environmentalism* included a more comprehensive, ecological vision of a vast web of life in which humans were more connected and vulnerable than they had imagined. Whereas Teddy Roosevelt had been trying to save the Grand Canyon, environmentalism was trying to save humans from themselves, which might require some deeper questioning of modern society.

America's national parks benefited from this new energy, but they were also caught unprepared for it. A century had now passed since the railroad had arrived at Yellowstone and started defining national parks as good backdrops for luxury hotels. Providing tourist services had become a central part of NPS culture. The Mission 66 building surge had not stopped in 1966; at Grand Canyon National Park it would continue into the early 1980s.

There had always been ecologically minded people inside the NPS, but usually they were playing the role of critics and not planners. Yet through the 1960s the groundwork was being laid for a redefinition of NPS values. In 1963 a group of independent scientists led by biologist A. Starker Leopold (the son of Aldo Leopold) issued the Leopold Report, which critiqued the NPS's lack of ecological research, perspectives, and policies; it would become something of a constitution for the environmental era to come. In 1964 Congress passed the Wilderness Act, which protected wilderness areas and wildlife habitat for their own sake, not because they served any human uses; it represented a shifting center of gravity in the conservation movement.

The Leopold Report and the Wilderness Act illustrated the varied sources and forces that would act upon Grand Canyon National Park in the decades to come. Some, like the Leopold Report, came from scientists and NPS leaders rethinking old values. Others, like the Wilderness Act and the Endangered Species Act of 1973, came from national legislation. Some forces came from within the park itself; others came from conflicts on the local, regional, and interagency levels.

The rise of environmental thinking coincided with the climax of Mission 66, whose problematic results forced even tourism-minded park managers to confront the paradoxes and futility of the situation. The environmental movement also gave park managers some support and freedom they had not had before. Ideas that had seemed too controversial, such as banning cars from park roads and replacing them with mass transit, were now easier to sell to Congress and the public. Setting limits on the numbers of backpackers and river runners on the grounds of "preserving the wilderness experience" might disappoint the college kids with *Walden* in their backpacks, but they understood the goal of having a wilderness experience. Park boundaries and policies that had been drawn up without regard for ecological realities might now be subject to renegotiation.

After the emergence of the environmental movement, the main story at Grand Canyon and other national parks has been the incorporation of ecological thinking and environmental values into park policies. This process has been complicated and discontinuous, full of starts and stops and retreats and new directions. It depended on layers of agencies and leaders, from the president downward, who were changing frequently, sometimes sharing the same values, sometimes conflicting. Yet overall it continued moving forward, driven by an evolution of cultural values.

The Grand Canyon had continued attracting writers who were precursors and shapers of cultural trends, and in the 1950s and '60s the canyon was prompting writers to ponder environmental questions.

In 1929 Joseph Wood Krutch, a Columbia University literary scholar, stirred up national controversy with his book *The Modern Temper,* which held that science had destroyed the traditional foundations of human dignity and goodness and that nature is absurd and monstrous. The book closed with the line "Ours is a lost cause and there is no place for us in the natural universe." The next year, on a national train trip to promote his book, Krutch started reading Thoreau's *Walden.* Through Thoreau's eyes Krutch began seeing nature as a source of meaning. Being humble before nature did not make humans "a lost cause"; a humble attitude was actually correct and healthy. Krutch wrote an admiring biography of Thoreau and began writing his own literary nature books. When Krutch retired in the early 1950s, he moved to Arizona. Like Harriet Monroe and John C. Van Dyke, Krutch struggled to adjust his perceptions to the desert. He did okay with small things like cacti and birds, but the Grand Canyon posed a larger challenge. In *The Modern Temper* Krutch had portrayed humans as tiny and insignificant before nature, and this idea seemed proven by the Grand Canyon. In his 1958 book, *Grand Canyon: Today and All Its Yesterdays,* Krutch repeatedly called the canyon "the abyss," the term intellectuals were using for existential meaninglessness. The canyon brought out tugs between Krutch's old and new visions of nature: "What it would mean to live always so precariously perched on the edge of such vast splendor I cannot imagine. . . . But to be always a mere speck—something, let us say, like an ant crawling up a cathedral—might be more than the human spirit could endure for long. Our littleness is something we need to be reminded of fairly frequently. But it would be hard to have to face up to it day after day and year after year."[1] Yet like John Muir, Krutch was calling the canyon "a cathedral." And he found the canyon compelling precisely because it enforced human humility, the essential foundation for environmental values.

In his book Krutch used the canyon as a platform for teaching ecological ideas. Krutch pointed out that the canyon's cliffs consisted of the fossils of extinct species that had not been able to adapt to environmental stress. He prescribed canyon humility: "Actually we are suffering from delusions of grandeur, from a state of hubris which may bring about a tragic catastrophe in the end. And I cannot imagine how we may be cured of it if the only effect of coming face to face with the most impressive demonstrations of what nature can do ... is an intensification of the delusion that she has been conquered and outdone."[2]

Whereas for Krutch environmentalism was at heart a philosophical issue about the place of humans in nature, for Wallace Stegner it was all about history. As a novelist Stegner won the Pulitzer Prize and the National Book Award, but he was also a historian, and his novels were mainly about the power of history over human lives and national values. The American conquest of the West had been such a great success story in economic and national terms that it left Americans blind to the damage it had done to nature, human lives, and community values. Stegner was born in fertile Iowa but grew up on the much drier western plains, and he watched settlers struggling and failing because they were blindly trying to carry out the settlement practices that had worked farther east. This drew Stegner's attention to John Wesley Powell, who in 1877 had tried to warn Americans about the realities of the arid West. In 1953 Stegner published *Beyond the Hundredth Meridian,* which chronicled Powell's explorations of the Colorado River and resurrected his largely forgotten environmental efforts. Stegner's book was an intellectual landmark that called for history to be examined from an environmental viewpoint. Stegner was also one of the directors of the Sierra Club, and in the 1960s he helped lead the fight against the Grand Canyon dams.

Stegner taught writing at Stanford, and one of his students was Edward Abbey. Stegner and Abbey did not hit it off. In his personal values and novels Stegner emphasized the importance of the human community. Edward Abbey was an anarchist at heart, for whom human civilization was inherently corrupting. Yet Abbey fitted the Thoreau mold of rejecting a materialistic society in favor of nature, so soon his *Desert Solitaire* (1968) was being stashed into backpacks alongside *Walden*. Throughout his long college years Abbey worked in national parks, including at Grand Canyon; he was a ranger at Lees Ferry and a fire lookout on the North Rim. He arrived in the peak years of Mission 66 and was disgusted by the emphasis on "industrial tourism," on paving the wilderness. Some of his Grand Canyon adventures were included in *Desert Solitaire*. In his writings Abbey did not take himself seriously and was ready to play the fool and provocateur, but he was serious about taking environmental ideas out of the classroom and personifying them in the vividly real world of deserts and canyons. Abbey had fallen in love with river trips through deep canyons, which made Lees Ferry—the launching place for Grand Canyon trips—a logical place for him to work. Yet he arrived there shortly after Glen Canyon Dam, fifteen miles upstream from Lees Ferry, had choked off the Colorado River to let its reservoir fill. The river was now a pitiful remnant of its old power. River lovers try to come up with material reasons that dams are bad (they hurt native fish and so forth), but at heart it is a philosophical matter, a dislike of seeing ancient and powerful rivers strangled for human uses. In 1975 Abbey published *The Monkey Wrench Gang*, a novel whose characters set out to free the Colorado River by blowing up Glen Canyon Dam. Yet Abbey did not care that such an act would cause a flood that would do catastrophic damage to the Grand Canyon. The novel brought out the weakness of the 1960s countercultural attraction to environmentalism, which could have little to do with loving nature for its own sake. All along, Abbey the anarchist had been using nature as a mere symbol of human freedom.

From its diverse sources, environmentalism added up into a force that would reshape policies at Grand Canyon National Park. But the park's first major effort to push ecological values turned into a major public relations disaster.

Today Grand Canyon National Park is the best place in North America to see desert bighorn sheep. Yet in 1900 biologists were predicting that desert bighorns were doomed to extinction. After 1870 desert bighorn populations across the West plunged, driven down by hunting, habitat loss, and especially exposure to diseases from domestic sheep. But there was one place where extreme isolation had left the desert bighorn population largely intact: the Grand Canyon. In his 1916 park plan Aldo Leopold had said, "The importance and value of this herd of sheep can barely be over-estimated, since it is the largest remaining herd of mountain sheep in the United States."[3] But Leopold noted that the canyon's population of burros, left by prospectors, was growing and outcompeting the bighorns, and he urged aggressive action to defend the bighorns—by shooting the burros.

Bighorns had survived the Ice Age in the canyon, but they were falling to the Wild West, to relics of the era of conquering nature for the sake of wealth. The burros were doing far more damage to the canyon than miners ever had. Burros were natives of Africa, introduced to America by the Spanish, and they were a poor fit for southwestern ecosystems; they devoured the vegetation and guarded springs against other wildlife.

In 1924, even as the NPS was behaving nonecologically by killing predators and introducing nonnative fish, rangers began shooting burros, 1,467 of them through 1931. This was two and a half times the 600 bighorns estimated to be in the canyon. Superintendent Miner Tillotson thought the problem was solved, so he relaxed the park's efforts, but the burro population took off again. The culling began again, 370 burros by 1956 and 771 more between 1956 and 1968. All this was done rather secretly. Aldo Leopold had realized that shooting burros was politically dangerous: "Tourists might criticize the killing of these wild burros.... [T]he killing must therefore be handled carefully."[4] The public viewed burros as not just cute animals but Wild West icons.

In 1952 author Marguerite Henry arrived at the canyon determined to write a novel about Brighty, the North Rim burro of thirty years before. Superintendent Harold C. Bryant—the ecologist—did his best to discourage Henry from romanticizing burros, but she went ahead, and in 1967 her book became a movie. Wild burros were finding a political constituency: in 1972 a federal law made it a felony to kill a wild burro (though this did not apply inside national parks); it was only a misdemeanor to kill a bighorn sheep. In 1969, in response to public protests, park managers discontinued killing burros, and the burro population began growing again.

In 1972 Grand Canyon National Park got a new superintendent, Merle Stitt, who, like Harold C. Bryant, saw things ecologically. The park got lucky that it was Stitt who presided over the beginning of the environmental era, for Stitt was a biologist with degrees in forestry and wildlife management from the University of Michigan. By the 1970s it had become quite rare for a biologist to become superintendent of a major national park; as parks had gotten larger, they demanded skills for managing politics, people, budgets, and construction, but not ecosystems. In World War II Stitt had seen ecosystems as a matter of life and death: in the US Navy he trained sailors in survival skills for Pacific islands; in 1948 a *National Geographic* hypothetical article about getting stranded on a Pacific island featured a photo of Stitt eating some exotic fruit. Whereas Bryant had seen biology as a source of inspiration, Stitt saw it as a call for action. Some of the environmental initiatives of the 1970s had been given direction by Stitt's predecessor as superintendent, Robert Lovegren, but Stitt pressed them forward.

Stitt pushed to solve the burro problem permanently. He probably overestimated the degree to which ecological thinking had replaced Wild West sentiments. When word got out that rangers were planning to start shooting burros—to murder friendly old Brighty—there was outrage. The park received twelve thousand hostile letters, many filled with obscenities.

In the end, the park sent in cowboys on horses to round up the burros and herd them into inner-canyon corrals. Burros were dangled under helicopters and airlifted out of the canyon, and others were taken out on large motorized rafts. It was all extravagantly expensive, one thousand dollars per burro. The burros were put up for adoption. In the 1980s it was still rare to see bighorn sheep along the Bright Angel Trail, but gradually they became familiar sights.

Like most other famous national parks, Grand Canyon National Park was established for the sake of its geological landmarks and scenic vistas. Parks were happy to have some biological "stars" like Yellowstone's bears and bison, but the public saw them in terms of entertainment, not ecosystems. Merle Stitt had to spend a lot of the popularity of Grand Canyon National Park to implement ecological policies. In the years and decades to come, the NPS became increasingly committed to ecological thinking, to defending native species and actively opposing invasive species. This included rolling back damage the NPS itself had inflicted; by the 2010s the park was removing trout from canyon side streams.

When the Endangered Species Act passed in 1973, one of the first species listed as endangered was the humpback chub, which had lived in the Colorado River throughout the Grand Canyon until Glen Canyon Dam turned the river too cold for them—but left a small remnant population in the still-warm waters of one tributary, the Little Colorado River. The Endangered Species Act provided both obligations and resources for agencies such as the NPS, and within a few years the park was trying to save what was left of the native fish. The park could not do anything about river temperatures, but after studying chub ecology the park decided they could be successfully transplanted to other side streams, giving them a better base for long-term survival.

When Congress passed the Wilderness Act in 1964, some NPS leaders resented it as an intrusion on their bureaucratic turf; the NPS had been creating wilderness areas through administrative decisions, but the Wilderness Act gave wilderness areas their own legal authority and mandates. Merle Stitt welcomed the ecological values of the Wilderness Act and recommended that 92 percent of Grand Canyon National Park be designated as wilderness. This would ban motorized recreation from those areas, including from the Colorado River, where many commercial raft trips depended on motors. Another big controversy enveloped Stitt. Rafting companies persuaded Congress to protect the use of motors on the river. The wilderness designation never went through, though the NPS would manage much of the canyon as de facto wilderness.

In the year Stitt arrived at the park, 1972, more than sixteen thousand people took river trips through the canyon, more than in the first one hundred years (1869–1969) combined. All that traffic was hurting the ecosystem and the experience itself. The river was no longer a natural system but an artificial one controlled by Glen Canyon Dam upstream, which had cut off the supply of new sediments for maintaining beaches against the Colorado's substantial erosive powers. The dam's outflows fluctuated greatly every twenty-four hours to meet electricity demands in Phoenix, and this increased beach erosion. In 1973 Stitt began the Colorado River Research Program, which lasted three years and brought in teams of scientists to study twenty-nine aspects of river ecosystems and human impacts. The result was a series of regulations to make river use fit river reality; they included limiting trip numbers, spacing out launches to avoid overcrowding, and requiring trips to haul out all wastes. The park began trying to get the Bureau of Reclamation to run Glen Canyon Dam with greater regard for downstream impacts. Grand Canyon also became one of the first national parks to require permits for backpackers, which set limits on numbers and camping locations and required "leave no trace" practices.

Stitt established a new department just to conduct scientific and environmental research in the park. This and other initiatives required securing major funding increases for the park, which in 1970 was receiving only a fraction of the funding received by Yosemite; Grand Canyon had as many or more visitors than Yosemite, but California had more than ten times the population and political clout of Arizona.

Stitt's era brought an ecological perspective to the problem of forest fires. A half century after foresters and park rangers had accepted predators like mountain lions as a necessary part of the ecosystem, they were still regarding forest fires as tree predators that needed to be ruthlessly suppressed. This policy had disrupted the natural fire cycle in which every few years small fires, ignited by lightning, burned up the fallen branches, pine needles, baby trees, and grasses on the forest floor but left the mature trees unharmed. Without fires, fuels accumulated for decades, and when fires came they quickly became catastrophic wildfires that raced for miles. The solution was to set periodic "prescribed burns" to replace natural fires and to thin out the now grossly overgrown forests. The North Rim, with its more extensive forests, became the park's proving ground for new forestry practices. To educate the public about evolving fire policies, fire crews appeared at evening ranger programs, in clothing still smoky from their day's work. One North Rim fire-crew chief was Stephen Pyne, who would go on to write many books about the history and ecological role of forest fires. At this time the North Rim's fire lookout was Edward Abbey, but park rangers joked that if Abbey's own fire tower caught fire, he might not even notice.

In the 1970s there were days when twenty-eight thousand people were jamming South Rim roads that the Santa Fe Railway had designed for buggies. Merle Stitt joked that he had to go to Phoenix to get away from traffic congestion. In 1974 Grand Canyon again became a trendsetter among national parks by offering mass transit. The chronically jammed Hermit Road was closed to private cars during summer and left accessible only through buses. Another (but voluntary) bus route circled Grand Canyon Village. Most riders appreciated being able to relax, enjoy the view, hear the driver's narration, and start friendly conversations with other travelers, but some people complained that banning cars was un-American.

The Clean Air Act of 1970 sought to clean up America's polluted skies, mainly for public health reasons, but it also recognized the value of scenic enjoyment. Amendments in 1977 and 1979 gave this goal some legal teeth, designating "Class One" areas—including Grand Canyon National Park— that should be free of impaired visibility. The Grand Canyon had a serious air-pollution problem, partly from smog blowing all the way from Los Angeles but mainly from two regional coal-fired power plants, especially the Navajo Generating Station. When environmentalists had defeated the two dams proposed for the Grand Canyon, the dams were replaced by the Navajo Generating Station, whose groundbreaking ceremony was held on April 22, 1970 — the original Earth Day. The plant, a few miles from Glen Canyon Dam, generated nearly twice as much power as the dam, and it was also the biggest source of the haze that cut visibility at the Grand Canyon by more than half. The canyon was more of a visual experience than most national parks, and it was one of the most important parks, so other parks looked to Grand Canyon to take the lead at testing the powers of the new clean-air laws. In 1979 the park began a program to monitor air quality and to identify pollution sources. The resulting political dance became very complicated, with numerous agencies and environmental groups squaring off. The NPS was only one of several agencies within the Department of the Interior, and it was seriously outranked by the Bureau of Reclamation — the agency behind Glen Canyon Dam and one of the agencies behind the Navajo Generating Station — which generated a lot of revenue and political clout. But in the end the Grand Canyon was deemed worth the $420 million it cost to install emissions scrubbers on the Navajo Generating Station.

The environmental era also provided the boost that finally got park boundaries expanded to include the entire canyon, 1.2 million acres, a bill signed by President Gerald Ford on January 3, 1975. In his youth Ford had been a park ranger in Yellowstone, but he had never been to the Grand Canyon, and after his retirement he and his wife, Betty, drove their RV to the park, where a ranger gave them a personal tour.

The Senate sponsor of the park expansion bill, Arizona's Barry Goldwater, had a unique bond with the canyon. In 1940, at age thirty-one, Goldwater had become the seventy-second person to take a river trip through the canyon. He took a lot of photos, and afterward he made a tour of Arizona to lecture about his canyon trip. The Goldwaters were the state's leading mercantile family, owners of the major department store in Phoenix and trading posts on Indian reservations, and Barry's tour made him a popular figure and led to his career in politics. As a senator Goldwater regularly — but futilely — introduced bills to expand the park's boundaries. For the 1975 bill Goldwater went to bat for the Havasupai, who were seeking to regain their ancestral lands; because of their trading posts, the Goldwaters had strong ties with Native Americans. The Havasupai were opposed by the NPS and the Sierra Club, which feared the precedent of removing lands from the public domain and giving them to any private entity. In a curious mix-up of stereotypes, environmentalists, who usually idealized Native Americans as land stewards, were opposing tribal rights, and Barry Goldwater, who might wear a cowboy hat while giving a speech celebrating the American frontier spirit, was championing the Indians—who won.

While the Havasupai felt that the NPS had failed them in their land dispute, the 1970s also began a new era in park-tribal relations. The American Indian Religious Freedom Act of 1978 required federal agencies to at least consult tribes about how new policies and actions might impact them or things of cultural importance to them. Grand Canyon National Park began to reach out to the tribes. By the 1990s the park was taking tribal leaders down the river so they could relate the cultural and religious significance that canyon places or ruins held for them. The park would bar river runners from visiting several places sacred to the tribes.

The 1970s also brought greater respect for historic preservation. In 1974 the park reviewed its historic buildings and designated a Historic District—including El Tovar and Hopi House—that would later be promoted to a National Historic Landmark.

Merle Stitt's retirement in 1980 coincided with the start of a national political climate that reembraced the old American view of the land as a resource for exploitation. Stitt had encouraged interpretive rangers to discuss environmental issues in their public programs, but now rangers were told to avoid controversy and stick to pretty rocks and wildflowers. Yet environmentalism now had major legal tools to support it, and by the end of the 1980s the canyon had several environmental organizations devoted to it, most important the Grand Canyon Trust and Grand Canyon River Guides.

The National Environmental Policy Act of 1970 had mandated an environmental impact statement for federally funded construction projects. In 1982 new plans for the generators at Glen Canyon Dam prompted an environmental impact statement to study how dam operations were impacting the Grand Canyon downstream and how they might be altered. The Glen Canyon Environmental Studies project did extensive scientific research, including some pioneering hydrology on the fundamental dynamics of rivers, especially how rivers build or erode sandbars. The goal was to make the most of a river system now starved of sediment. The result, in 1996, was a dramatic experimental flood; the dam was opened up to let out several times the river's normal flow, to excavate sediment from the riverbed and deposit it onto beaches. In 1992 Congress passed the Grand Canyon Protection Act, requiring that Glen Canyon Dam could no longer be operated solely to maximize electricity or profits but had to be operated in a way that minimized harm to Grand Canyon ecosystems.

By the 1980s air tours over the canyon had become a multimillion-dollar business involving forty-five companies and a quarter of a million customers per year. Mather's and Albright's dislike of air tours had never become policy. In the 1970s the park began an Aircraft Management Plan, but the park had no authority to regulate commercial or private flights, since the airspace over national parks was controlled—actually, uncontrolled— by the Federal Aviation Administration. Military jet pilots were roaring through the canyon for stunts. Private and commercial pilots were flying anywhere they wanted, right to the canyon bottom, right over the heads of hikers, bighorn sheep, and Havasupai in their village. Flights were dangerously random, with aircraft popping out from behind cliffs and mesas and the rim, going every direction, buffeted by the canyon's strong winds. In the two decades before 1986 there had been ten crashes inside the canyon, with 41 deaths, and many more crashes on the rim near the canyon. None were midair collisions between two sightseeing aircraft, but to park managers it was obvious this was just a matter of time. The time came in June 1986: a sightseeing airplane and helicopter collided and fell into the canyon, killing 25 people. The next year Senator John McCain—whose navy-pilot heroism gave him high credibility on an aviation issue—won passage of the National Parks Overflights Act, which gave the NPS the authority to regulate the airspace above parks. Grand Canyon National Park used its new authority to establish a flight pattern over the canyon, a large one-way loop that allowed aircraft to keep an eye on one another; flights were no longer allowed below the rim.

In the year Bill Clinton was elected president, 1992, visitation to Grand Canyon National Park jumped to more than 4.5 million, up from 3.9 million the year before and 3.5 million five years before. Clinton's secretary of the interior, Bruce Babbitt, was very aware of the automobile traffic problems plaguing the park. The Babbitt family was to northern Arizona what the Goldwaters were to southern Arizona, the leading mercantile family,

FIGURE 9.1. From the 1950s onward, parking lots were chronically jammed. In the 1990s Interior Secretary Bruce Babbitt, whose family owned the park's general store seen in this photo, tried to expand mass transit in the park, but Congress blocked his plans.

owners of the major department store in Flagstaff and trading posts on Indian reservations. In 1910 the Babbitts had opened the grocery store at the South Rim. By the 1980s the parking lot for their expanded store was clogged with cars and RVs all summer. Bruce Babbitt, who had published two books about the Grand Canyon, took the park's problems personally and was determined to solve the traffic problem by greatly expanding the park's mass transit system. Most visitors would be required to park outside the national park boundary and take light-rail trains into the park, where they would board shuttle buses for touring the rim. This plan reflected a major change in NPS philosophy, which called for limiting new developments inside parks and building new services on or outside park boundaries. The park started building the train and bus station near the rim, but then a more conservative Congress arrived and axed funding for the trains. Now the park had a train station but no trains. The station was also the park's new Visitor Center, so now the welcoming rangers were stranded in the middle of nowhere, with no parking lots, and visitors who wanted to visit the Visitor Center had to walk there from Mather Point, where there was not nearly enough parking, forcing cars to sprawl along the shoulders of the road for a half mile. It took years for the park to pick up the pieces, which required creating massive parking lots for the Visitor Center and running a voluntary shuttle system from there.

In 1989 a private company made a quicker contribution to mass transit by rebuilding the long-abandoned railway from Williams to the South Rim and restarting daily passenger trains, which headed off hundreds of cars from clogging park roads and lots.

Bruce Babbitt also got President Clinton to add three new national monuments adjoining the park, which gave the Grand Canyon more coherence as an ecosystem.

The most dramatic act of ecological restoration at the Grand Canyon was for the California condors, the largest birds in North America. Condors had been living at the canyon as late as 1881, when a prospector shot the last one. A century later their total population was down to only twenty-two, and they seemed guaranteed to go extinct. Wildlife biologists rounded up the remaining condors and placed them in a captive breeding program, which proved quite successful. In 1996 six condors were released at the Vermilion Cliffs just north of the Grand Canyon. Within five years condors were nesting inside the canyon—inside caves that held condor bones from centuries ago.

The environmental era reinvigorated Grand Canyon art, after decades in which the art world, pursuing the abstract and pop, dismissed landscape art as uncool. Environmental perspectives influenced visions of the canyon. An increasing number of artists had grown up in the Southwest or had spent a lot of time exploring the canyon from the inside, and for them doing justice to the canyon was not about Pretty; it was about Power. For hit-and-run artists on the rim, the canyon remained merely a visual experience, distant and safe. For hikers and river runners, the canyon was an intense and personal experience, an immersion in raw and powerful elements, in rocks and waves and heat and thunderstorms, overwhelming and dangerous. It was a sign of the times that the canyon artists who won the largest followings were those offering insider visions of the canyon's power.

Ed Mell painted his Grand Canyon paintings in a studio three blocks from the Phoenix hospital where he was born—you cannot get much more rooted than that. Yet in between, Mell moved to New York City and worked for an advertising agency, made a lot of money, and was miserable. As a break one summer he returned to Arizona and taught art in a Hopi village. He decided to return to Arizona. The designs Hopis use on their pottery and jewelry are very elemental, like the geometry of mesas and canyons. Mell's Grand Canyon paintings were similar: very elemental, simplifying the landscape into its basic geometry and colors. Art critics might call this abstraction, but at sunset the Grand Canyon really does lose its details and melts into fundamental shapes and colors, glows and shadows. Mell was bringing out the canyon's real strengths.

Among river runners the most popular artist was Serena Suplee, a river guide based in Moab, Utah, who rowed the Grand Canyon many times. Like Ed Mell, she left out details to bring out fundamentals, and she exaggerated colors to suggest the intensity of the experience. Most of her paintings were from the river's viewpoint, with waves curving through O'Keeffe-sinuous cliffs.

When it came to being a canyon insider, no one could compete with Bruce Aiken, who for three decades lived at Roaring Springs inside the canyon, running the pumps that supplied water to the rims. He had fled New York City to paint the West. Park managers figured it would be easier to train a bohemian painter to be a pump-house operator than to find a plumber who could tolerate living in such an isolated spot. Aiken and his wife, Mary, raised three children there, homeschooling them. Aiken carried his paintings out of the canyon on his back. He had a better opportunity to study the canyon in all its moods and details than any previous artist, though increasingly he was impressed by how well Gunnar Widforss had done. Many of Aiken's paintings were inner-canyon scenes, which were not always appreciated by people who recognized the canyon only from rim views. He was especially good at river scenes, at capturing the sheen of water and the energy of rapids. Yet he felt that no one could ever really do justice to the canyon. For him, painting the canyon was a way of praising the ultimate painter, God.

The river experience also generated the only work of Grand Canyon music that ranks alongside Ferde Grofé's *Grand Canyon Suite:* Paul Winter's 1986 *Canyon.* Like Grofé's work, Winter's was rooted in jazz and offered a suite of Grand Canyon scenes and events. But whereas Grofé offered a tourist's experience of the canyon, and while his clip-clopping mules had classified his work as a piece of Americana, Winter offered a rafter's experience, and he was seeking deeper connections with nature. Winter and his

FIGURE 9.2. Artist Bruce Aiken (*right*) spent more than three decades operating the inner-canyon pump house to have a unique chance to paint the canyon.

musicians took four river trips through the canyon, played music in its side canyons, and sought the canyon's musical heart. Two sections depicted the act of rafting, one with joy, the other with terror.

If the environmental era can be defined as an attempt to see nature from the inside and to find the right balance of humility, strength, and joy, there was no better place to do this—artistically, musically, or philosophically—than in the Grand Canyon. Yet in spite of the progress, some problems seemed interminable, and at the start of the twenty-first century the big picture was discouraging. The desert Southwest has always been a marginal environment, with regular droughts, with plants, wildlife, and humans already living on the edge of survival. The Grand Canyon is littered with the ruins of a society that was swept aside by drought. The threat of climate change was more serious for the Southwest than for most places, with the potential to wipe out forests and dry up the Colorado River, already overtaxed by the growth of southwestern cities. Whether the Grand Canyon, and the environmental protections it has gained, can withstand the tremendous pressures of climate change remains to be seen.

The environmental era also showed some diminished perceptions of the Grand Canyon. For the first generation to see the canyon, human technology was epitomized by the train on which they had arrived; the world had not yet been shrunken by airplanes, automobiles, rockets, television, the Internet, global climate change, and the atomic bomb. The canyon had overwhelmed humans and human pride. The environmental era perceives a world and a canyon being overwhelmed by human civilization. Humility is no longer the obvious response to the canyon; now all the plaques with scoldings from John Muir and Teddy Roosevelt are lucky to make some people pause in their rush to Hoover Dam and Las Vegas. The ecological "harmony of nature," a balance of predators and prey, of pollution and government regulations, was a weak substitute for the romantics' nature-mediated harmony between humans and God. A canyon swarming with helicopters, rafts, and hikers seemed more about recreation than Creation.

CHAPTER TEN

Adventure

The Mount Everest of River Trips

Every year tens of thousands of people come to the Grand Canyon not for its geology, beauty, Native American heritage, or pioneer history, but because they are seeking the greatest adventure of their lives. For river runners and backpackers, the canyon is one of the world's ultimate destinations. A boating trip down the Colorado River, taking two weeks or more, is an intense immersion in wilderness and test of whitewater skills—river runners everywhere have heard of Lava Falls. Hiking in the canyon tests the endurance and skills of hikers who feel at home in the Rockies or Alps. Even tourists who will never leave the rim know that the canyon is famous for adventure, and they look for rafts on the river and hikers on the trails.

Today's adventurers are following in the footsteps of people for whom the canyon was a different sort of adventure. For Native Americans, the canyon was home, more than it would ever be for today's rangers or river runners. They were born of the canyon, and their lives were upheld by its sacred meanings. For them, hiking the canyon's sketchy routes—the forerunners of today's trails—was all about going home or finding food or honoring shrines or visiting sisters in the next drainage. They wandered into remote areas—leaving their projectile points—that today's hikers seldom see. They also must have tied together some logs and rafted the Colorado River, at least enough to cross it on their seasonal migrations in and out of the canyon, and perhaps some brave youths headed through rapids. Perhaps a real adventure gave rise to the Hopi story of Tiyo, who rode through the Grand Canyon in a hollow log and won the secret of bringing rain and life to his people. The canyon continues to give life to people today.

Euro-American adventurers brought to the canyon their own long history and cultural values. For some, it was all about conquering the wilderness; the canyon was a trophy that proved their superiority over nature and other people. Others were drawn to the canyon because they were seeking primordial power and beauty. The same cultural forces, the same contest between conquest and reverence, that animated the rest of Grand Canyon history was active in the rich history of canyon adventures.

John Wesley Powell's boyhood reads like a map of Manifest Destiny: his family moved from New York to Ohio to Illinois, and in his postcanyon Washington career he played a significant role in encouraging settlement of the West. He understood the American mystique of the heroic explorer and enjoyed wrapping himself in it. Yet the geologist in him never stopped seeing the canyon's grandeur. Powell could be forgiven for not seeing poetry in a river that was doing its best to kill him, but he ended his book with a tribute to it: "The river thunders in perpetual roar, swelling in floods of music when the storm gods play upon the rocks.... Thus the Grand Canyon is a land of song. Mountains of music swell in the rivers, hills of music billow in the creeks.... The adamant foundations of the earth have been wrought into a sublime harp."[1] Powell set an example to the generations of river runners who would idolize him and sit in camp reading his book out loud. Powell made it okay for macho river runners to have a poetic side.

Yet when Frederick Dellenbaugh wrote his history of the second Powell expedition, it was a young man's tale of action and conquest. The river was "the enemy," against which "we set forth for another day's battle," and "we felt that we were vanquishing the Grand Canyon with considerable success."[2]

In 1909, forty years after Powell's journey, Julius F. Stone's expedition marked the transition between the eras of exploitation and adventure. Stone was an Ohio industrialist who became the financial backer of Robert Stanton's 1890s scheme of building a dredge to extract gold dust from the gravel bars of Glen Canyon. Stone came to inspect the dredge preparations and got a 125-mile ride through Glen Canyon, guided by Nathaniel Galloway, who was working for Stanton. Stone was enthralled.

Stone became the first person to hire a guide—Nathaniel Galloway—to take him through the Grand Canyon for the sheer joy of it. Camped at the canyon's first rapid, Stone loved the moonlight on the cliffs and how the canyon was "uplifting and swaying the beholder with a sense of being that is delightful past compare."[3]

In 1897 Nathaniel Galloway had been the fourth person to launch a Grand Canyon river trip, and he had added key innovations in boat design and rowing technique. Powell's and Stanton's boats had keels and little "rocker" (bottom curvature), which left most of the boat embedded in the water and hard to maneuver. Their crews rowed in the centuries-old style of rowboats, with the boat pointed downstream and the men with their backs to the rapids, peeking over their shoulders. Their rowing only added more speed to the boat, which was hardly necessary—and sometimes a bad idea—on the swift Colorado. More crucial than speed was control. Nathaniel Galloway designed his boats without a keel, with the bottom flat from side to side but more curved from front to back, making boats easier to turn. He went into rapids stern first, facing the rapid. He angled his boat so that either backstrokes or forward strokes could avoid obstacles. Backstrokes also allowed him to cut his speed. Galloway's technique was not entirely original, but he perfected it; from then on, river runners could actually run rapids and not avoid them.

Beginning with the second Powell expedition, cameras became an essential part of Colorado River trips. Powell's cameras were as unwieldy as his boats, but photography and canyon boating were evolving during the same decades and both had captured the public imagination. Julius Stone took along a photographer who took two thousand photos. Two years previously, prospector Charles Russell launched a three-boat trip that he claimed was for prospecting but that was also for taking photos Russell could sell to newspapers. The trip went badly and ended with only one boat and no photos.

In 1911 brothers Ellsworth and Emery Kolb started down the Green and Colorado Rivers with photography as their main purpose. Originally from Pittsburgh, roaming west for adventure, the Kolbs had arrived at the canyon just in time for the arrival of the Santa Fe Railway and mass tourism. They set up a photography business at the head of the Bright Angel Trail, taking souvenir photos of mule riders, but from their adventuresome spirit they roamed and photographed remote corners of the canyon. Movies were a new craze, and the Kolbs took a movie camera down the river to film their adventure. "We could not hope to add anything of importance to the scientific and topographic knowledge of the canyons . . . ," wrote Ellsworth, "and merely to come out alive at the other end did not make a strong appeal to our vanity. We were there as scenic photographers in love with their work."[4] Yet their book and movie were mainly about the adventure of going down the river, with only a few pauses to admire the canyon's scenery. They had their share of misadventure: hitting rocks, getting tossed overboard, flipping boats, smashing a hole in one boat, ruining some of

FIGURE 10.1. Emery Kolb, his wife, Blanche, and Ellsworth Kolb, at the original Kolb Studio, 1904. A decade later, after the brothers' river trip, they added an auditorium for showing their movie of their adventure.

their film, and running low on food. They benefited from the accumulated experience of canyon boaters and built Galloway boats and rowed them Galloway style, and they felt confident enough to run almost every rapid, though they portaged Lava Falls.

The Kolbs took their movie on a national tour, including Carnegie Hall. Then they added a small auditorium to their house and showed their movie there for the next six decades, narrated by Emery more than thirty thousand times, the longest-running movie in world history. Yet the Kolbs also did a disservice to Grand Canyon river running, making it seem a fun, harmless adventure and giving it a Hollywood flavoring. They would be imitated by several expeditions that were motivated mainly by publicity and that forgot the river-running lessons of four decades.

Envious of the Kolbs, Charles Russell tried again in 1914, this time with a movie camera and with steel boats that might resist collisions with rocks but otherwise were poor designs for the Colorado. He tempted fate by naming one boat *Titanic II*. Fate was not amused: the *Titanic II* escaped and went downstream without them; another boat got stuck in Crystal

Rapid and dumped all their cameras and film into the river. Russell gave up and hiked out of the canyon; within a few years, he was confined to an insane asylum.

The 1920s was the era of airplane stunt flying, and it was echoed by stunt boating. In June 1927 (only five weeks after Lindbergh's conquest of the Atlantic) Clyde Eddy launched a trip that would be remembered mainly for a crew that included a bear cub named Cataract and a dog named Rags. Eddy ignored decades of boat evolution and reverted to Powell's design.

In World War I Eddy had fought at the nightmare Battle of Verdun. Two years after the war he came to the Grand Canyon on his honeymoon, stood before Hermit Rapid, and was enthralled by its power and danger: "There is my river," he thought. Combat, not poetry, was his attitude toward the canyon. The river was a dragon and "a wicked devil." A huge rock in the river was "like Cerberus guarding the gates of hell."[5] He lay awake at night listening to the roar of rapids and recalling the roar of explosions at Verdun. For a crew he had sought out college students, the same age as the soldiers he had fought with, though he also sought out Parley Galloway, the well-trained son of Nathaniel Galloway, as a guide.

During a bad run in Hance Rapid, Eddy "had looked over the side of the boat into the whirling, churning water and knew that I had looked into the face of ... death." They wrecked one of their three boats in Deubendorff Rapid. Rapids gave Eddy both fear and "the pure joy of conflict." Yet this joy had a therapeutic, even philosophical dimension: "The constant presence of danger gives richness to life—where the daily threat of death makes clear how good it is to live. No man who keeps to the beaten path can ever know the joy of home-coming after a long absence."[6] Eddy's use of the Colorado River as the water equivalent of war invites comparison with John Wesley Powell. Shiloh was Powell's Verdun, and he seems to have found his own test and catharsis on the river. But Powell also found far more than the devil and hell in the canyon. (Rags the dog got left behind at one beach, but both he and the bear made it through.)

A few months after Eddy's trip, a Hollywood movie company launched a trip to film a melodrama. They too took a dog mascot, Pansy. The river inflicted many mishaps and miseries, including December cold that left the crew coated in ice, and at the Bright Angel Trail several people quit— even Pansy quit. The film's climax was at Hermit Rapid, where the prop of an airplane wing was carried down the Hermit Trail on mules and perched in the rapid—a plane wreck. The big rescue scene went wrong when a boat that had been nearly sawed in half to allow it to break on a rock actually failed to break, and another boat missed its route and plunged into a hole and flipped, leaving the rider—a boatman dressed in a skirt and blond wig to be the stunt double of the heroine—with a bloody face and crooked wig. The film was never released, and later it disappeared.

The next year, 1928, Glen Hyde, a twenty-nine-year-old from Idaho, came up with a trip mascot even better than a bear cub or a dog—his wife, Bessie. He and Bessie would go down the Colorado River as their honeymoon trip, making Bessie the first woman to run the river, enabling them to make a vaudeville/lecture tour, a book, and some money. In Idaho Glen had operated an unusual boat called a sweep scow, a long wooden trough without any oars on the sides but with two long rudders on the bow and stern. This design worked well enough on a river with a steady gradient and a moderate volume, but it would prove grossly clumsy on the Colorado River. Glen built a scow twenty feet long and five feet wide, with sweep oars twenty feet long. Proud of his ability as a swimmer, Glen refused to take life jackets. Launching in Utah, they made it through the huge rapids of Cataract Canyon, but by the time they were a third of the way into the Grand Canyon and hiked up the Bright Angel Trail and met with Emery Kolb, Bessie seemed unnerved. Kolb offered them life jackets, but Glen refused. They were last seen running Hermit Rapid. When they failed to arrive below the Grand Canyon, a rescue search located their boat a dozen miles below Diamond Creek, still upright, in good shape, still holding their supplies, including Bessie's diary. River historians suspect that the Hydes collided with the rocks in 232-Mile Rapid and were thrown overboard and drowned. Bessie had gotten within fifty miles of being the first woman to complete a Grand Canyon river trip.

A decade later, and nearly seventy years after Powell, someone finally did everything right. Buzz Holmstrom was born in a world of rivers and boats, near the Oregon coast, in 1909, the year Julius F. Stone became the first person to run the Colorado River for the love of it. Twenty-eight years later, in 1937, Holmstrom achieved the first solo trip through the Grand Canyon in a boat he named the *Julius F* in honor of Stone, who admired Holmstrom's spirit and donated five hundred dollars to support his journey. Holmstrom went for the love of it, and in his river journal he wrote about the canyon with the heart of a poet. In spite of the dangers, he felt a deep harmony with the river, the canyon, the starry sky. There was also a lot of harmony in the boat he designed and in the way he rowed it. Holmstrom was largely self-taught as a boat builder and oarsman. He studied river history and designed a Galloway-style boat but modified it significantly, making it stronger and more stable and maneuverable. Six decades later veteran river guide and historian Brad Dimock built a replica of Holmstrom's boat and rowed it through the Grand Canyon and decided it was the best design he had ever rowed.

Holmstrom was also a keen judge of rapids, able to assess the dynamics of currents and waves and to direct his boat exactly where he needed to go. In the canyon he portaged only one rapid, Lava Falls. Near the end of his trip, when other oarsmen would have been feeling quite proud of themselves, Holmstrom penned some words that have become a favorite quote for river runners who feel that humility is the only correct answer to the canyon:

I find I have already had my reward—in the doing of the thing—the stars & cliffs & canyons—the roar of the rapids—the moon. . . .

I think this river is not treacherous as has been said—Every rapid speaks plainly just what it is & what it will do to a person & a boat. . . . If only one will read & listen carefully—it demands respect—& will punish those who do not treat it properly . . . but many people do not believe what it says. . . .

Some people have said "I conquered the Colorado Riv—I don't say so—It has never been conquered—& never will I think—anyone who it allows to go thru its canyons & see its wonders should feel thankful & privileged. . . .

I know I have got more out of this trip by being alone than if a party was along as I have more time—especially at nite—to listen & look & think & wonder about the natural wonders rather than listen to talk of war politics & football scores. . . .

The Riv probably thot—he is such a lonesome ignorant unimportant & insignificant pitiful little creature—with such a short time to live that I will let him go this time & try to teach him something—It has not been so kind to many prouder people than I.[7]

Holmstrom's achievement caught the respect of fellow Oregonian Amos Burg, who had run several major rivers and written about his trips for *National Geographic.* Burg had wanted to run the Colorado, so he persuaded Holmstrom to repeat his trip the next year, 1938, with Burg along to film it. Burg gave Holmstrom the safety margin to run every rapid, making him the first person to do so. Burg was a kindred spirit who called the canyon "splendid desolation," enjoyed the beauty of the night sky above the cliffs, and felt humility. When Burg's movie company insisted on titling his film *Conquering the Colorado,* both Holmstrom and Burg were appalled.

Burg brought something new to the Colorado River: a rubber raft. Burg designed his own raft, sixteen feet long with twenty-six airtight compartments, and persuaded a skeptical rubber company to manufacture it. Burg knew his raft was an experiment, and he had some rough rides and lined Lava Falls, but his success opened the door—halfway—to the future of river running.

The door was opened the other halfway only ten weeks before Holmstrom and Burg launched their trip. Norm Nevills, who operated a lodge in Mexican Hat, Utah, and who had been taking a few paying passengers down the San Juan River, became the first person to take passengers through the Grand Canyon. He started the fourth era of canyon river running; after exploration, exploitation, and adventure, the era of commercial river running would make the canyon available to large numbers of people.

Nevills's 1938 trip was commissioned by a University of Michigan botanist named Elzada Clover, who wanted to study the canyon's plants, and she brought along her student Lois Jotter. They became the first women to complete a Grand Canyon river journey.

Nevills's boats were his own design, wider and flatter than Galloway boats and with little room for passengers, who had to cling to the deck. Nevills lined the worst rapids; wooden boats remained vulnerable to hitting rocks. It took fourteen years after the 1938 debut of rubber rafts and commercial trips for someone to combine the two ideas in a big way.

Georgie White was an adventuresome woman. At age twenty-five, in 1936, she and her husband rode bicycles from New York City to Los Angeles, where they settled. Georgie loved hiking in the California mountains and deserts. She was riding bikes with her daughter, Sommona, when a car hit and killed Sommona; Georgie's grief nearly drove her mad. Then she attended a Sierra Club lecture by Grand Canyon adventurer Harry Aleson, and her grief clicked into an obsession with the canyon. The next year she and Aleson attempted to swim the lower Colorado River from Havasu down, and when this proved a bad idea, they rafted the lower river in a six-foot rubber raft. Hooked, she bought an army-surplus seven-man raft, and

FIGURE 10.2. Norm Nevills led the first commercial river trip in the Grand Canyon in 1938. Behind him is the bridge on the South Kaibab Trail.

after getting some experience she took it down the Grand Canyon in 1952, becoming the first woman to row a boat through the canyon. Soon she bought old army bridge pontoons and tied them together to make a raft thirty-three feet long, with a lot of room for paying passengers. She continued running trips for four decades, until a few months before her death. Other companies sprang up and improved her raft design.

The advent of rubber rafts nearly ended the era of wooden boats, but

FIGURE 10.3. Georgie White launched commercial rafting in
the canyon in the 1950s.

in the early 1960s journalist Martin Litton became fascinated by Oregon's
wooden dories, with their wave-rocking upswept bows. Litton was an envi-
ronmentalist firebrand who would help lead the opposition to the proposed Grand Canyon dams, and to him rubber rafts seemed as unnatural
as dams; wood was nature's own medium. Starting in 1947 Moulty Fulmer
had mutated the Nevills boat toward the dory, and Litton continued mold-
ing dories to fit the Colorado's big water and started a company to run dory
trips. In 1983, as Lake Powell overflowed into a flood through the canyon,
three dory boatmen set a canyon speed record of thirty-six hours.

The Inuit had used kayaks for thousands of years, but only at the start
of the twentieth century did kayaking become a whitewater sport, first in

Europe. In 1907 Hans Klepper in Germany began producing "foldboats" with a rubberized canvas cover and a wooden frame, foldable into two suitcase-size bags. In only three decades foldboats showed up on the Colorado River.

In 1938 two French men and one woman launched their kayaks from Green River, Wyoming, carrying all their own supplies. Genevieve DeColmont became the first woman to pilot a boat of any kind down the Colorado. Her husband, Bernard, worked for the Paris Museum of Natural History and was filming southwestern canyons, and he wanted to prove that kayaks worked best for wilderness expeditions. When they applied for permission to kayak through the Grand Canyon, they met the kind of skepticism that kayakers would encounter for another quarter century: the NPS demanded that they make a ten-thousand-dollar deposit to pay for the inevitable rescue party. Their trip went pretty well, with a few hard knocks, but by the time they were approaching Lees Ferry in November the bitter cold was filling the river with little icebergs. The kayakers waited three weeks, hoping for warmer weather, and finally gave up.

Three years later a champion American kayaker, Alexander "Zee" Grant, persuaded a highly skeptical Norm Nevills to take him through the Grand Canyon; Nevills agreed only if Grant signed away any blame for his injury or death. Grant was a severe diabetic and gave himself insulin shots all through the canyon. Nevills saved a space on one boat for when Grant destroyed his kayak. When Grant arrived and Nevills asked him where his kayak was, Grant held up two bags, and Nevills gave him a cold, disheartened stare.

The foldboat manufacturer too was skeptical that their boats could survive the Grand Canyon, so Grant designed a special boat, a sixteen-foot "rubber battleship" with a river-dynamic shape and side pontoons made from the inner tubes of New York City buses.

Grant got off to a terrible start. As he approached the first rapid, Badger, he discovered that the drop was so steep he could not see where he was, and in spite of Nevills's frantic signaling from shore, Grant went straight into Badger's worst hole, which pulled him from his boat and popped his inflatable rubber life jacket. At the third rapid, House Rock, Grant imagined he could maneuver away from its huge waves, but he was swept down the main current, flipped, and knocked out of his boat again. Nevills was appalled, imagining a long nightmare trip, or a quick drowning. Yet Grant was a quick learner, and he spilled only one more time, although he carried his boat around the worst rapids, like Lava Falls.

One of Nevills's passengers was Agnes Albert of California, who came from old pioneer stock and was a hardy adventurer. She took a turn in Grant's kayak and became the first woman to paddle a kayak in the Grand Canyon, if on flat water and riffles. The first women known to have done some serious kayaking were on a 1970 trip organized by kayaking ace Walt Blackadar, who invited, among other women, Barbara Wright, the champion racer who had taught him how to kayak. Wright ran only part of the river, but this included Crystal and Lava Falls. In 1991 Sharon Hester, a veteran raft guide, made a solo kayaking trip through the canyon, calmly running everything.

For Alexander Grant, kayaking the Colorado River was all about adventure; in the article he wrote about his trip, he offered no admiration for the canyon. Two decades later, for the next man to kayak the canyon, it meant a lot more.

Walter Kirschbaum grew up in Germany in the 1920s, with kayaking booming as a sport, and he got started at age fourteen. In World War II Kirschbaum was drafted into the Nazi army and fought on the Russian front, where he was captured and spent years in a brutal prison camp. Kirschbaum survived physically but not emotionally: he emerged raw and desolated. His anxiety and desolation found a therapeutic outlet in kayaking, and he pursued it ferociously. Within a few years he won the world championship in kayak racing. Winning races gave him some sense of worth, but not enough to fill his void. In 1955 he came to the United States to compete in the national championship races on Colorado's Arkansas River, above where it flowed through the Royal Gorge. In Europe Kirschbaum had seen Alpine chasms, but there was something different about desert canyons, with their ancient, surrealistic cliffs. Their grandeur made his demons smaller; their peace began seeping into him. Racing was all about proving superiority over other people, but canyons were about feeling humility before nature. "I began to enjoy exploring remote rivers more than racing," he wrote in an article about his 1960 Grand Canyon journey. "I found wilderness canyons so attractive that all the success I had had in slalom and downriver races of national and international level faded

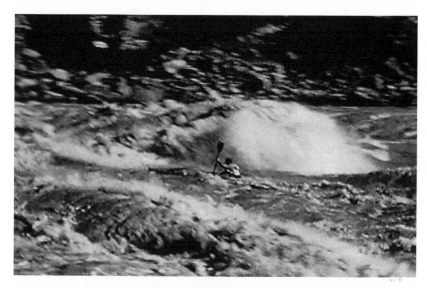

FIGURE 10.4. Almost invisible amid the giant waves of Lava Falls, Walter Kirsch-baum became the first person to kayak the world's most famous rapid in 1960. (From movie taken by Dr. Yuji Oishi.)

in importance compared to the deep impulses experienced on my excursions. . . . [C]anyon expeditions give far more and deeper satisfaction."[8]

When Kirschbaum sought permission to run the Grand Canyon, the NPS first refused and then required him to prove his abilities by first kayaking Cataract Canyon in Utah, though its hardest section is harder than any comparable mileage in the Grand Canyon. Even after he passed this test, the NPS told him to portage Lava Falls.

In June 1960 Kirschbaum headed into the Grand Canyon on high water, forty thousand cubic feet per second, paddling a handmade fiberglass kayak with a canvas cover—and no seat or internal braces, which he felt were unnatural. He wore no helmet or life jacket. He ran every rapid, including Lava Falls.

In Hance Rapid he got knocked over. "I tried twice to recover, but failed due to the sweeping power of these haystacks. A giant's fist, then, it seemed, dragged me out of my kayak. I . . . found myself being whirled around in circles. . . . [T]he whirlpools never seemed to end, and when one of them released me another was waiting to take over."[9]

In spite of the stress, Kirschbaum felt a deep contentment in the canyon; he treasured this adventure more than any other. After the canyon he set out to run all of the Colorado River's tributaries. Yet he never escaped his demons. He began drinking too much. A decade later, in his home in Santa Fe, he fell asleep in the bathtub, and he drowned.

Like John Wesley Powell and Clyde Eddy, the war-wounded Walter Kirschbaum found a catharsis on the Colorado River. Their daring might also suggest men who had once counted themselves as already dead. Driven to a rematch with the fate that had overwhelmed them, driven to seek a powerful antidote to gloom, they emerged from the Grand Canyon with a new sense of ability and life. At the end of his canyon journey, Powell had a flashback to his Civil War nightmare, with a prison image that could have come from Kirschbaum's prison nightmare:

> The relief from danger and the joy of success are great. When he who has been chained by wounds to a hospital cot until the canvas tent seems like a dungeon cell, until the groans of those who lie about tortured with probe and knife are piled up, a weight of horror on his ears that he cannot throw off, cannot forget . . . when he at last goes out into the open field, what a world he sees! How beautiful the sky, how bright the sunshine, what "floods of delirious music" pour from the throats of birds, how sweet the fragrance of earth and tree and blossom! The first hour of convalescent freedom seems rich recompense for all pain and gloom and terror.
>
> Something like these are the feelings we experience to-night. . . . Now the danger is over, now the toil has ceased, now the gloom has disappeared, now the firmament is bounded only by the horizon, and what a vast expanse of constellations can be seen!
>
> The river rolls by us in silent majesty. . . . [O]ur joy is almost ecstasy.[10]

In 1978 a Kirschbaum protégé, Fletcher Anderson, made a solo marathon run through the canyon in only forty-nine hours to Diamond Creek, a kayaking record that stood for nearly four decades. Stunned with exhaustion and pain, he once hallucinated that he saw the dead Walter Kirschbaum paddling alongside him.

Like most kayakers, Kirschbaum and Anderson were adrenaline addicts who enjoyed conquering rapids, but they also felt a deep humility, one they shared with Powell, Holmstrom, and Burg. This humility came partly from risking one's life against an overpowering nature, but it was also the humility of reverence. The intensity and character that made these men the pioneers of Grand Canyon river running, that inspired the greatest risks and innovations, also left them ready to experience the canyon with a greater spirit, to appreciate it for all the right reasons.

Both river running and backpacking soared in popularity in the late 1960s and 1970s, partly because of the "back to nature" youth culture and also because good equipment—especially for river runners—was becoming much more available.

As with river running, the first decades of canyon hiking were all about exploitation, about prospectors searching for wealth. The first generation of tourists came from a preautomobile America where most people knew how to ride horses, so most tourists relied on mules to reach the canyon depths. Hiking remained an unnecessary, somewhat eccentric activity.

But a few bold people began hiking the canyon for the sake of exploration and adventure. In 1902 François Matthes of the US Geological Survey made heroic treks to create the first thorough topographical map of the canyon. In Washington, DC, Matthes was the leader of a Boy Scout troop that included Eddie McKee, who went on to a great career as a Grand Canyon ranger, including heroic treks for the sake of natural history. The Kolb brothers lugged their cameras into remote areas for the sake of photography. Starting in the 1920s Allan MacRae, a bespectacled theology professor from Pennsylvania, began leaving canyon trails to find his own routes, and he probably ran into God along the way. In 1939 Merrel Clubb, a bespectacled English professor from Kansas, became enthralled with the canyon and began exploring its backcountry and making first ascents of its peaks. In 1945 Harvey Butchart, a bespectacled math professor from nearby Flagstaff, started the twelve thousand miles of hiking—including numerous new routes and first ascents of peaks—that would make him the most famous of canyon hikers.

It does not take a bespectacled professor to notice a trend here. Devoting decades to exploring the canyon's most difficult passageways is indeed a somewhat eccentric activity, and it requires a special motivation—like intense curiosity. John Wesley Powell was the original canyon professor (if without spectacles) for whom curiosity rivaled his survival instinct. For Harvey Butchart, who was only the first of several math nerds who became famous canyon hikers, finding new routes was an equation to be solved.

Like river runners, hikers brought varied personalities and values to the canyon. Some of the college students who hiked with Butchart became frustrated by his need to arrive at a goal as quickly as possible (the word *adventure* comes from the Latin *to arrive*), not stopping to smell the wildflowers and see the rocks, ruins, and grand vistas. Butchart's problem-solving attitude was also a contrast with Merrel Clubb, who felt a more spiritual bond with the canyon, especially for places whose names came right out of his field of medieval literature—Merlin Abyss, Wotan's Throne.

In 1962, when Butchart had hiked most of the canyon's length in numerous short hikes and segments, he heard from Colin Fletcher, a writer from Berkeley, California, who announced his plan to through-hike the canyon's length—or at least the length of the national park, which was still barely half of the canyon's geological length. Butchart had always regarded his canyon feats as trophies that proved his worth, and his competitive impulses were triggered by Fletcher's plans, so he went out and completed his last segment. Fletcher could not understand Butchart's hit-and-run attitude in which the canyon was, in Fletcher's words, "an obstacle course, to be covered, defeated."[11] Butchart could not understand Fletcher's hope of using his canyon hike to immerse himself in geological and evolutionary time.

Colin Fletcher's 1967 book, *The Man Who Walked Through Time,* chronicled not just his physical adventure but his perceptual and philosophical quest: "The eons before man emerged were not a terrible void, were not something my mind had to shun.... To understand man's significance, I saw, you must first accept his insignificance. Only then could you focus him into importance against his stupendous, unshruggable background."[12]

Fletcher's book offered some of the best-yet writing about how the canyon could allow humans to feel within themselves the vastness of geological time and the long, creative flow of life. Fletcher did for hikers what Powell had done for river runners, defining the Grand Canyon as a landscape that was humbling yet deeply meaningful. Through Powell and Fletcher, the canyon had managed to break through the clamor of American history, of a nation's proud striving for wealth and greatness, and to speak eloquently of its own realities.

Conclusion
The Land Was Ours Before We Were the Land's

From here, you can see forever.

I was looking at the Grand Canyon through the large windows on the top level of the Desert View Watchtower. To the east I was looking high over the canyon rim and into the Painted Desert. Ninety miles away I saw Navajo Mountain, where in the 1860s the Navajos had tried to hide from the cruel tide of American national expansion; the other main area where they hid was right here, this part of the canyon's South Rim. I saw the gorge of the Little Colorado River winding toward the Grand Canyon. I saw the Colorado River, miles of it, the best view of it from any tourist overlook.

When the Santa Fe Railway selected a spot on the rim to build its train station and lodges, it selected an area from which the river was hidden from view. They probably did not anticipate how much tourists would enjoy spotting the river, and besides, this was the easiest route for the tracks. Three decades later Mary Colter, in building the Desert View Watchtower, paid better homage to the river's inspirational power.

Colter was also paying homage to the Hopis and their vision of the canyon as a sacred place of creation. She took pains to make the Watchtower look like an authentic Ancestral Puebloan tower, although paradoxically this meant adding a lot of fake details, such as a large crack running through the wall. And paradoxically, in the same years the Santa Fe Railway was giving Colter the money and artistic freedom to honor Native Americans, it was shoving the Hualapais aside to get control of their springs.

The Watchtower's rustic stones conceal a sturdy concrete foundation and steel skeleton, built by the contractor that built bridges for the Santa Fe Railway. The railway and its bridges were built to conquer the wilderness and expand the American nation. In the Midwest the Santa Fe had bridged the mighty, flood-prone Mississippi. In the Rockies it had bridged and tunneled its way through Raton Pass. In the Southwest it had bridged canyons hundreds of feet wide and deep. Its toughest challenge was bridging the Colorado River on the Arizona-California border. Its first Colorado River bridges, in the 1880s, were knocked down by floods. In 1890 the Santa Fe built the world's largest cantilever bridge, but the river continued undermining it, allowing the bridge to sag several inches under the weight of trains. In 1942, with the Colorado River's floods now controlled by Hoover Dam upstream, today's bridge at Topock was built.

As I stood atop the Watchtower's vertical bridge, I saw that the Colorado River, running green and not its ancient red, had also been tamed by a dam above the Grand Canyon. I spotted little colored dots on the river, rafts, with guides—at least some of them—convinced they were conquering the river. The American conquest of nature looked pretty complete.

Yet in the year the Desert View Watchtower was built, 1930, the American culture of runaway growth and greed had gone badly wrong, bringing down the stock market and starting the Great Depression. The same steel mills that produced the Santa Fe's bridges had also made the plows and tractors that broke a prairie that for millennia had been scuffed only by buffalo hooves and teeth; Americans tried to force the land to grow too much with too little water, and now the prairie had become the Dust Bowl, sending clouds of Oklahoma soil all the way to New York, sending crowds of Oklahomans to California.

Some Oklahomans packed all their possessions onto their rusty trucks and headed west on Route 66, still refusing to give up the American Dream of a better life in the West. Others had no trucks or possessions and hopped rides on freight trains. They rode Santa Fe trains across Arizona, across the bridge that had conquered the Colorado River. Like all the railroads, the Santa Fe hired watchmen, whom the hobos called "bulls," to keep hobos off trains; some bulls were sadists who would happily push a man to his death.

One freight-riding Okie, whose only possession was his guitar, was troubled by the failure of the American land and the American Dream. He was annoyed when he heard Irving Berlin's new song "God Bless America," which saw only natural beauty and not Dust Bowls, only God-given blessings and not human-made inequities. In rebuttal he wrote his own song, "God Blessed America," musically based on an old Baptist hymn, in which God's blessings had been seized and ruined by greedy men and corporations. His original refrain was "God blessed America for me." Then he crossed out this line and replaced it with "This land was made for you and me." Then he changed the title, taking it from the song's first line: "This land is your land, this land is my land."

Woody Guthrie's ballad sprang from America's long groping for identity, from the tension between its democratic ideals and its all-out rush for wealth. Guthrie's lines embodied Mark Twain's moral outrage against the Gilded Age, Teddy Roosevelt's conservation values, and ongoing efforts to coax American values away from their powerful individualism and toward a greater sense of community. His song embodied the core idea of the national parks. As these values gained further momentum in the decades to come, Guthrie's song would be deemed worthy of becoming a new national anthem.

Guthrie's lines belonged to the first part of Robert Frost's transition: "The land was ours before we were the land's." Yet Guthrie was thinking about the second part, how we could belong to the land. In 1936 he spent some time in Santa Fe and became enthralled by pueblo-style buildings, made from adobe, from the land itself. He wandered through the Santa Fe Railway's pueblo-style La Fonda Hotel, designed with help from Mary Colter, and admired its murals of Pueblo Indian life. He went out to a Pueblo village, centuries old, where people spent their lives rooted to the nurturing earth where they were born, and he painted oil paintings of it. Later, he wrote a novel centered around adobe architecture, *House of Earth*, admiring it not aesthetically but philosophically, for the idea that humans could live inside the land. Adobe houses also fitted his populist values, for anyone could build them, free of bank mortgages. Guthrie's character says, "I'll be one that'll never take to the road that goes nowhere. I can stand out there in this yard on a clear day and see the spot where I was born."[1]

When Mary Colter built the Desert View Watchtower, she was thinking about how the Hopis saw the land as their birthplace, not just personally but spiritually. To the Hopis, the Grand Canyon was not just an "our land" public park or an aesthetic spectacle, but a spiritual landscape that connected them with the depths of creation, the mysteries of life and death. To paint the Watchtower murals she could have selected a famous white artist and gotten the kind of romanticized images of Indians that Americans preferred, but instead she selected a Hopi, Fred Kabotie, from a family that had led the fight against assimilation into American ways, to paint in traditional Hopi "folk" style. Next to his mural showing the story of Tiyo,

FIGURE C.1. *Desert View Watchtower,* by Gunnar Widforss, ca. 1932, watercolor on paper, 13 x 20 inches (33 x 51 cm). Photograph courtesy of a private collector.

Kabotie painted a rainbow that bridges the sky, bridges the daily route traveled by the sun between two kivas.

Breaking through the powerful, proud American national story; rising against the juggernaut that had flattened the land, forests, wildlife, and people; wearing the very skeleton of conquest—the Grand Canyon was making its own power heard.

While the spiritual world of the Hopis might be quite different from the scientific worldview, they did share a powerful image: human life had emerged from the depths of the Grand Canyon. To scientific eyes, the canyon's geological pages tell the story of massive forces that move continents, raise mountains, build miles of rock, lift seafloors into high plateaus, and carve canyons. The canyon rocks tell the story of cells evolving into more complicated forms and toward human forms. Although the scientific vision was not as personal as the Hopi vision of souls returning to the canyon to reach the afterlife, it could still emerge from abstract ideas into very personal realities. The ancient seawater that had built the canyon cliffs was still flowing in human veins and killing hikers who failed to keep their salt equation balanced. The Cambrian tracks in the Bright Angel Shale had turned into human footprints on the moon and into cathedral windows with angels. The forces that had sculpted canyon cliffs had also sculpted human faces. The canyon depths offered a mirror in which humans could see their own depths, see how "we were the land's."

When the science of ecology matured, it added a new layer of human connections with the land and other species, not in the past but in the present, not an evolutionary connection but a living economy, requiring humility. Once again science—which had provided the tools and encouraged the arrogance for conquering nature—had arrived at a vision that shared a lot with the vision of Native Americans.

In the 1920s, only a few years before the Desert View Watchtower was built, a famous astronomer, George Ritchey, dreamed of building the world's greatest astronomical observatory right here. Ritchey and his partner, George Hale, had built Mount Wilson Observatory, where Edwin Hubble would prove that the universe is expanding. Ritchey and Hale began dreaming of building a greater observatory, and Ritchey became obsessed with the idea that it needed to be built on the rim of the Grand Canyon. Ritchey should have recognized that the turbulent air at the canyon rim made it a terrible place for astronomy. Yet Ritchey drew up plans for a classical-style observatory tower about twenty-five stories tall. Ritchey seems to have become enthralled with the canyon as a revelation of the same ancient forces of creation he was seeking in the night sky. George Hale, who was now a rival and planning his own observatory atop Palomar Mountain, was so spooked by Ritchey's Grand Canyon plan that he sent Edwin Hubble to the canyon to test it as an observatory site.

Ritchey's observatory was never built, but it may have helped inspire Mary Colter to build the Desert View Watchtower on the same spot a few years later. She believed that Ancestral Puebloan towers had served partly as astronomical observatories; she directed Fred Kabotie to paint many Hopi astronomical motifs.

This was indeed an excellent place from which to view the expanding universe. I could follow for miles the expanding gorge of the Little Colorado River and imagine in it the Sipapuni, the Hopi's Big Bang. Yet long before the canyon had found human minds and voices to give it poetry and meaning, the canyon had proclaimed the mystery of cosmos, Earth, and life.

Then, in the recent rush of human events, John Wesley Powell had arrived at the junction of the two rivers, saw the Grand Canyon through the map of the unfolding American nation, and declared it to be "the great unknown." In only thirty years it was thoroughly absorbed into the American story of wilderness conquest. But the canyon would not remain absorbed, for its own story was too powerful. It appealed to the ideals of a democratic nation and became a "land made for you and me." It appealed to the need of an urban, disconnected world to remember what the earth had always been. It appealed to the unending human need for origins, for some sort of sacredness, and became a rock-framed window to the cosmos. It went from being "the great unknown" of national dreams to the philosophical "great unknown" of human wonder.

Notes

INTRODUCTION

1. Robert Frost, *Collected Poems*, 348.

ONE. GEOLOGY

1. J. S. Newberry, *Geological Report*, 45 (emphasis in the original).

2. John Wesley Powell, *The Exploration of the Colorado River and Its Canyons*, 263, 390–93.

3. John C. Van Dyke, *The Grand Canyon of the Colorado*, 15; Mary Austin, *The Land of Journeys' Ending*, 421.

4. Clarence E. Dutton, *Tertiary History of the Grand Cañon District*, 141–42.

5. J. Van Dyke, *Grand Canyon of the Colorado*, 81–82.

6. Quoted in Donald Worster, *A Passion for Nature: The Life of John Muir*, 376; John Muir, "The Grand Canyon of the Colorado."

7. John Burroughs, "The Grand Canyon of the Colorado."

8. Quoted in Don E. Wilhelms, *To a Rocky Moon: A Geologist's History of Lunar Exploration*, 202.

THREE. EXPLORERS

1. George Parker Winship, trans. and ed., *The Journey of Coronado, 1540–1542*, 116.

2. Elliot Coues, trans., *On the Trail of a Spanish Pioneer: The Diary and Itinerary of Francisco Garcés in His Travels Through Sonora, Arizona, and California, 1775–1776*, 351.

3. Ibid., 347.

4. James Ohio Pattie, *The Personal Narrative of James Ohio Pattie of Kentucky*, 97.

5. Earle Spamer, "Once Again, 'Who Named the Grand Canyon?'—and Other Grand Canyon 'Firsts,'" 4.

6. Joseph C. Ives, pt. 1, "General Report," in *Report upon the Colorado River of the West, Explored in 1857 and 1858 by Lieutenant Joseph C. Ives*, 71.

7. Ibid., 81–82.

8. Ibid., 99, 100.

9. Ibid., 107, 111.

10. Ibid., 109, 110.

11. Ibid., 5.

12. Michael P. Ghiglieri, ed., *First Through Grand Canyon: The Secret Journals and Letters of the 1869 Crew Who Explored the Green and Colorado Rivers*, 191.

13. For a fuller discussion of this scenario, see Don Lago, "New Evidence on the Origins and Disintegration of the Powell Expedition," in *Reflections of Grand Canyon Historians: Ideas, Arguments, and First-Person Accounts*, edited by Todd R. Berger, 119–22.

14. J. W. Powell, *Exploration of the Colorado River*, 204.

15. Ghiglieri, *First Through Grand Canyon*, 198.

16. J. W. Powell, *Exploration of the Colorado River*, 247.

17. Ibid., 248.

18. Ghiglieri, *First Through Grand Canyon*, 207, 206; J. W. Powell, *Exploration of the Colorado River*, 251.

19. J. W. Powell, *Exploration of the Colorado River*, 264.

20. Ibid., 279–80.

21. For a complete discussion, see Don Lago, "The Toquerville Myth."

22. Frederick Dellenbaugh, *A Canyon Voyage: The Narrative of the Second Powell Expedition*, 237.

FOUR. EXPLOITERS

1. Robert Brewster Stanton, *Down the Colorado*, 152.

2. Robert Brewster Stanton, *The Colorado River Survey: Robert B. Stanton and the Denver, Colorado Canyon, and Pacific Railroad*, 141.

3. Dale L. Walker, *Rough Rider: Buckey O'Neill of Arizona*, 173.

FIVE. CONSERVATION

1. Stanton, *Down the Colorado*, 4.

2. Muir, "Grand Canyon of the Colorado," 107.

3. Theodore Roosevelt, speech given at Grand Canyon, May 6, 1903, quoted in *New York Sun*, May 7, 1903.

4. Theodore Roosevelt, *A Book Lover's Holiday in the Open*, 22.

SIX. CULTURE

1. C. F. Lummis, "The Greatest Thing in the World," in *The Grand Canyon of Arizona*, by Santa Fe Railway, 36.

2. Henry Van Dyke, *The Grand Canyon, and Other Poems*, 5–8.

3. J. Van Dyke, *Grand Canyon of the Colorado*, 3, 5, 218.

4. C. S. Gleed, "The Canyon by Dark and by Day," in *Grand Canyon of Arizona*, by Santa Fe Railway, 66; C. A. Higgins, "The Titan of Chasms," in ibid., 11; George B. Reeve in ibid., 117.

5. William Allan White, "On Bright Angel Trail," in ibid., 64–65.

6. Ibid.

7. Theodore Roosevelt in ibid., 117; John Muir, in ibid., 114.

8. C. B. Spencer in *Grand Canyon of Arizona*, by Santa Fe Railway, 113; John L. Stoddard, "A Gash in Nature's Bared Breast," in ibid., 38–41; Charles Dudley Warner, "On the Brink of the Canyon," in ibid., 89.

9. Harriet Monroe, *A Poet's Life: Seventy Years in a Changing World*, 165–66.

10. Harriet Monroe, "Its Ineffable Beauty," in *Grand Canyon of Arizona*, by Santa Fe Railway, 35–37.

11. George Sterling, "At the Grand Canyon," in *Sonnets to Craig*.

12. Quoted in William Drake, *Sara Teasdale: Woman and Poet*, 204.

13. Alfred Noyes, *The Book of Earth*, 14 (emphasis in the original).

14. Ibid., 11.

15. Ibid., 328.

16. Carl Sandburg, "Many Hats," in *The Complete Poems of Carl Sandburg*, 430.

17. Sandburg, "Slabs of the Sunburnt West," in ibid., 311.

18. Ibid., 310.

19. Sandburg, "Many Hats," 434.

20. This and following quotes from El Tovar "Impressions" books, Special Collections, Cline Library, Northern Arizona University, Flagstaff.

21. Thomas Moran, *Home Thoughts from Afar: Letters of Thomas Moran to Mary Nimmo Moran*, 33, 39; *Scribner's* quoted in Thurman Wilkins, *Artist of the Mountains*, 134.

22. Muir, "Grand Canyon of the Colorado"; Burroughs, "Grand Canyon of the Colorado"; Muir, "Grand Canyon of the Colorado."

23. Ferde Grofé, "Story of *Grand Canyon Suite*," 8.

24. J. B. Priestley, *Midnight on the Desert: Being an Excursion into Autobiography During a Winter in America, 1935–36*, 285.

25. Ibid., 286.

26. Ibid., 284–85.

SEVEN. NATIONAL PARK

1. Aldo Leopold and Don P. Johnston, "Grand Canyon Working Plan," 1917, GCRA 28344, Grand Canyon National Park Museum Collection.

2. C. A. Higgins, "The Titan of Chasms," reprinted in *Grand Canyon of Arizona*, by Santa Fe Railway, 13.

3. Leopold and Johnston, "Grand Canyon Working Plan"; Curt D. Meine, *Aldo Leopold: His Life and Work*, 160.

4. Meine, *Aldo Leopold*, 160.

5. Alfred Runte, *National Parks: The American Experience*, 93.

6. Miner Tillotson and Frank J. Taylor, *Grand Canyon Country*, 61.

7. John Steinbeck, *"America and Americans," and Selected Nonfiction*, 381–82.

EIGHT. ARCHITECTURE

1. Leopold and Johnston, "Grand Canyon Working Plan."
2. Virginia L. Grattan, *Mary Colter: Builder upon the Red Earth*, 111.

NINE. THE ENVIRONMENTAL ERA

1. Joseph Wood Krutch, *The Modern Temper*, 169; Joseph Wood Krutch, *Grand Canyon: Today and All Its Yesterdays*, 194.
2. Krutch, *Grand Canyon*, 26.
3. Leopold and Johnston, "Grand Canyon Working Plan."
4. Ibid.

TEN. ADVENTURE

1. J. W. Powell, *Exploration of the Colorado River*, 394–97.
2. Dellenbaugh, *Canyon Voyage*, 219, 220, 234.
3. Julius Stone, *Canyon Country: The Romance of a Drop of Water and a Grain of Sand*, 84.
4. Ellsworth L. Kolb, *Through the Grand Canyon from Wyoming to Mexico*, 3–4.
5. Clyde L. Eddy, *Down the World's Most Dangerous River*, 5, 164, 166.
6. Ibid., 121, 178, 188.
7. Buzz Holmstrom, *Every Rapid Speaks Plainly: The Salmon, Green, and Colorado River Journals of Buzz Holmstrom*, 114–15.
8. Walter Kirschbaum, "Grand Adventure," 6.
9. Ibid., 7.
10. J. W. Powell, *Exploration of the Colorado River*, 284–85.
11. Quoted in Elias Butler and Tom Myers, *Grand Obsession: Harvey Butchart and the Exploration of the Grand Canyon*, 258.
12. Colin Fletcher, *The Man Who Walked Through Time*, 213.

CONCLUSION

1. Woody Guthrie, *House of Earth: A Novel*, 209–10.

Bibliography

Abbey, Edward. *Desert Solitaire*. New York: Simon and Schuster, 1990.

———. *The Monkey Wrench Gang*. New York: HarperCollins, 2006.

Albright, Horace M. *The Birth of the National Park Service: The Founding Years, 1913–1933*. Salt Lake City: Howe Brothers, 1985.

Anderson, Michael F. *Along the Rim: A Guide to the Grand Canyon's South Rim from Hermit's Rest to Desert View*. Grand Canyon: Grand Canyon Association, 2001.

———, ed. *A Gathering of Grand Canyon Historians: Ideas, Arguments, and First-Person Accounts: Proceedings of the Inaugural Grand Canyon History Symposium, January 2002*. Grand Canyon: Grand Canyon Association, 2005.

———. *Living at the Edge: Explorers, Exploiters, and Settlers of the Grand Canyon Region*. Grand Canyon: Grand Canyon Association, 1998.

———. *Polishing the Jewel: An Administrative History of Grand Canyon National Park*. Grand Canyon: Grand Canyon Association, 2000.

Audretsch, Robert W. *Shaping the Park and Saving the Boys: The Civilian Conservation Corps at Grand Canyon, 1933–1942*. Indianapolis: Dog Ear, 2011.

Austin, Mary. *The Land of Journeys' Ending*. New York: Century, 1924.

———. *The Land of Little Rain*. Boston: Houghton Mifflin, 1903.

Babbitt, Bruce E. *Color and Light: The Southwest Canvases of Louis Akin*. Flagstaff, AZ: Northland Press, 1988.

———, ed. *Grand Canyon: An Anthology*. Flagstaff, AZ: Northland Press, 1978.

Barnes, Christine. *El Tovar at Grand Canyon National Park*. Bend, OR: W. W. West, 2001.

———. *Hopi House: Celebrating 100 Years*. Bend, OR: W. W. West, 2005.

Beattie, Donald A. *Taking Science to the Moon: Lunar Exploration and the Apollo Program*. Baltimore: Johns Hopkins University Press, 2001.

Belknap, Bill, and Frances Spencer Belknap. *Gunnar Widforss: Painter of the Grand Canyon*. Flagstaff, AZ: Northland Press, 1969.

Benson, Jackson J. *Wallace Stegner: His Life and Work*. Lincoln: University of Nebraska Press, 2009.

Berger, Todd R., ed. *Reflections of Grand Canyon Historians: Ideas, Arguments, and First-Person Accounts*. Grand Canyon: Grand Canyon Association, 2008.

Berke, Arnold. *Mary Colter: Architect of the Southwest*. New York: Princeton Architectural Press, 1997.

Billingsley, George H., Earle E. Spamer, and Dove Menkes. *Quest for the Pillar of Gold: The Mines and Miners of the Grand Canyon.* Grand Canyon: Grand Canyon Association, 1997.

Braine, John. *J. B. Priestley.* New York: Barnes and Noble, 1978.

Brian, Nancy. *River to Rim.* Flagstaff, AZ: Earthquest Press, 1992.

Briggs, Walter. *Without Noise of Arms: The 1776 Domínguez-Escalante Search for a Route from Santa Fe to Monterrey.* Flagstaff, AZ: Northland Press, 1976.

Brinkley, Douglas. *The Wilderness Warrior: Theodore Roosevelt and the Crusade for America.* New York: HarperCollins, 2009.

Burroughs, John. "The Grand Canyon of the Colorado." *Century Illustrated Monthly Magazine,* January 1911, 425–38.

Butler, Elias, and Tom Myers. *Grand Obsession: Harvey Butchart and the Exploration of the Grand Canyon.* Flagstaff, AZ: Puma Press, 2007.

Cahalan, James M. *Edward Abbey: A Life.* Tucson: University of Arizona Press, 2003.

Cahill, Daniel J. *Harriet Monroe.* New York: Twayne, 1973.

Carothers, Steven W., and Bryan T. Brown. *The Colorado River Through Grand Canyon: Natural History and Human Change.* Tucson: University of Arizona Press, 1991.

Carr, Ethan. *Mission 66: Modernism and the National Park Dilemma.* Amherst: University of Massachusetts Press, 2007.

Carroll, Sean B. *Remarkable Creatures: Epic Adventures in the Search for the Origins of Species.* New York: Houghton Mifflin Harcourt, 2009.

Chaikin, Andrew. *A Man on the Moon: The Voyages of the Apollo Astronauts.* New York: Viking, 1994.

Coder, Christopher M. *An Introduction to Grand Canyon Prehistory.* Grand Canyon: Grand Canyon Association, 2000.

Colter, Mary. *Manual for Drivers and Guides Descriptive of the Indian Watch Tower at Desert View and Its Relations, Architecturally, to the Prehistoric Ruins of the Southwest.* Grand Canyon: Fred Harvey, 1933.

Compton, Todd M. *A Frontier Life: Jacob Hamblin, Explorer and Indian Missionary.* Salt Lake City: University of Utah Press, 2013.

Cook, William. *The Wen, the Botany, and the Mexican Hat: The Adventures of the First Women Through Grand Canyon on the Nevills Expedition.* Orangevale, CA: Callisto Books, 1987.

Coues, Elliot, trans. *On the Trail of a Spanish Pioneer: The Diary and Itinerary of Francisco Garcés in His Travels Through Sonora, Arizona, and California, 1775–1776.* Vol. 2. New York: Francis P. Harper, 1900.

Courlander, Harold. *The Fourth World of the Hopis: The Epic Story of the Hopi Indians as Preserved in Their Legends and Traditions.* Albuquerque: University of New Mexico Press, 1971.

Cray, Ed. *Ramblin' Man: The Life and Times of Woody Guthrie.* New York: W. W. Norton, 2004.

Dellenbaugh, Frederick. *A Canyon Voyage: The Narrative of the Second Powell Expedition.* Tucson: University of Arizona Press, 1988.

Dimock, Brad. *Sunk Without a Sound: The Tragic Colorado River Honeymoon Trip of Glen and Bessie Hyde.* Flagstaff, AZ: Fretwater Press, 2001.

Dolnick, Edward. *Down the Great Unknown: John Wesley Powell's 1869 Journey of Discovery and Tragedy Through the Grand Canyon.* New York: HarperCollins, 2001.

Drake, William. *Sara Teasdale: Woman and Poet.* New York: Harper and Row, 1979.

Duncan, Dayton, and Ken Burns. *The National Parks: America's Best Idea.* New York: Alfred A. Knopf, 2011.

Dutton, Clarence E. *Tertiary History of the Grand Cañon District.* Tucson: University of Arizona Press, 2001.

Eddy, Clyde. *Down the World's Most Dangerous River.* Republished as *A Mad, Crazy River: Running the Grand Canyon in 1927.* Albuquerque: University of New Mexico Press, 2012.

Enote, Jim, and Jennifer McLerran, eds. *A:shiwi A:wan Ulohnanne: The Zuni World.* Zuni, NM: A:shiwi A:wan Museum and Heritage Center, and Museum of Northern Arizona, 2011.

Evans, Edna. *Tales from the Grand Canyon: Some True, Some Tall.* Flagstaff, AZ: Northland Press, 1985.

Fink, Augusta. *I-Mary: A Biography of Mary Austin.* Tucson: University of Arizona Press, 1983.

Fletcher, Colin. *The Man Who Walked Through Time.* New York: Random House, 1967.

Fried, Stephen. *Appetite for America: Fred Harvey and the Business of Civilizing the West—One Meal at a Time.* New York: Random House, 2010.

Frost, Robert. *Collected Poems.* New York: Henry Holt, 1979.

Ghiglieri, Michael, ed. *First Through Grand Canyon: The Secret Journals and Letters of the 1869 Crew Who Explored the Green and Colorado Rivers.* Flagstaff, AZ: Puma Press, 2003.

Goetzmann, William H. *Exploration and Empire: The Explorer and the Scientist in the Winning of the American West.* New York: Alfred A. Knopf, 1971.

Goodman, Susan, and Carl Dowson. *Mary Austin and the American West.* Berkeley: University of California Press, 2009.

Grattan, Virginia L. *Mary Colter: Builder upon the Red Earth.* Grand Canyon: Grand Canyon Natural History Association, 1992.

Grofé, Ferde. "Story of Grand Canyon Suite." *Arizona Highways,* December 1938.

Guthrie, Woody. *House of Earth: A Novel.* New York: HarperCollins, 2013.

Hagerty, Donald J. *Beyond the Visible Terrain: The Art of Ed Mell.* New York: Cooper Square, 1996.

Henry, Marguerite. *Brighty of the Grand Canyon.* Chicago: Rand McNally, 1953.

Hirst, Stephen. *I Am the Grand Canyon: The Story of the Havasupai People.* Grand Canyon: Grand Canyon Association, 2006.

Holmstrom, Buzz. *Every Rapid Speaks Plainly: The Salmon, Green, and Colorado*

River Journals of Buzz Holmstrom. Edited by Brad Dimock. Flagstaff, AZ: Fretwater Press, 2003.

Hughes, J. Donald. *In the House of Stone and Light: A Human History of the Grand Canyon.* Grand Canyon: Grand Canyon Natural History Association, 1978.

Ives, Joseph C. *Report upon the Colorado River of the West, Explored in 1857 and 1858 by Lieutenant Joseph C. Ives.* Washington, DC: US Government Printing Office, 1861.

Johnson, Michael L. *Hunger for the Wild: America's Obsession with the Untamed West.* Lawrence: University Press of Kansas, 2007.

Johnson, Robert Underwood. *Remembered Yesterdays.* Boston: Little, Brown, 1923.

King, Elbert. *Moon Trip: A Personal Account of the Apollo Program and Its Science.* Houston: University of Houston Press, 1989.

Kinsey, Joni Louise. *The Majesty of the Grand Canyon: 150 Years in Art.* Cobb, CA: First Glance Books, 1998.

——. *Thomas Moran and the Surveying of the American West.* Washington, DC: Smithsonian Institution Press, 1992.

Kirschbaum, Walter. "Grand Adventure." *American Whitewater* (November 1960).

Kolb, Ellsworth L. *Through the Grand Canyon from Wyoming to Mexico.* New York: Macmillan, 1914.

Krutch, Joseph Wood. *Grand Canyon: Today and All Its Yesterdays.* New York: Sloane, 1958.

——. *The Modern Temper.* New York: Harcourt, Brace, 1956.

Lago, Don. *Canyon of Dreams: Stories from Grand Canyon History.* Salt Lake City: University of Utah Press, 2014.

——. "The Toquerville Myth." *Boatman's Quarterly Review* (Fall 2003).

Lavender, David. *Colorado River Country.* Albuquerque: University of New Mexico Press, 1988.

——. *River Runners of the Grand Canyon.* Grand Canyon: Grand Canyon Natural History Association, 1985.

Leavengood, Betty. *Grand Canyon Women: Lives Shaped by Landscape.* Grand Canyon: Grand Canyon Association, 2004.

Mangum, Richard, and Sherry Mangum. *Grand Canyon–Flagstaff Stage Coach Line: A History and Exploration Guide.* Flagstaff, AZ: Hexagon, 1999.

Margolis, John D. *Joseph Wood Krutch: A Writer's Life.* Knoxville: University of Tennessee Press, 1980.

Martin, Tom. *Big Water, Little Boats: Moulty Fulmer and the First Grand Canyon Dory on the Last of the Wild Colorado River.* Flagstaff, AZ: Vishnu Temple Press, 2012.

Masters, Edgar Lee. *Across Spoon River.* New York: Holt, Rinehart, and Winston, 1936.

——. *Invisible Landscapes.* New York: Macmillan, 1935.

McFarland, Elizabeth. *Grand Canyon Viewpoints.* Phoenix: W. A. Krueger, 1978.

——. *This Is the Grand Canyon.* Phoenix: W. A. Krueger, 1970.

McGarry, Susan Hallsten. *Bruce Aiken's Grand Canyon: An Intimate Affair*. Grand Canyon: Grand Canyon Association, 2007.

Meine, Curt D. *Aldo Leopold: His Life and Work*. Madison: University of Wisconsin Press, 1988.

Monroe, Harriet. *A Poet's Life: Seventy Years in a Changing World*. New York: Macmillan, 1938.

Moran, Thomas. *Home Thoughts from Afar: Letters of Thomas Moran to Mary Nimmo Moran*. Edited by Amy O. Bassford and Fritiof Fryxell. East Hampton, NY: East Hampton Free Library, 1967.

Morehouse, Barbara J. *A Place Called Grand Canyon: Contested Geographies*. Tucson: University of Arizona Press, 1996.

Morris, Edmund. *The Rise of Theodore Roosevelt*. New York: Coward, McCann, and Geoghegan, 1979.

Muir, John. "The Grand Canyon of the Colorado." *Century Illustrated Monthly Magazine*, November 1902, 107–16.

Nelson, Nancy. *Any Time, Any Place, Any River: The Nevills of Mexican Hat*. Flagstaff, AZ: Red Lake Books, 1991.

———. *Theodore Rex*. New York: Random House, 2001.

Nevills, Norman D. *High, Wide, and Lonesome: The River Journals of Norman D. Nevills*. Edited by Roy Webb. Logan: Utah State University Press, 2005.

Newberry, J. S. *Geological Report*. Included in *Report on the Colorado of the West, Explored in 1857 and 1858 by Lieutenant Joseph C. Ives*, by Joseph C. Ives. Washington, DC: US Government Printing Office, 1861.

Niven, Penelope. *Carl Sandburg: A Biography*. New York: Charles Scribner's Sons, 1991.

Noyes, Alfred. *The Book of Earth*. New York: Frederick A. Stokes, 1925.

Osterbrock, Donald. *Pauper and Prince: Ritchey, Hale, and Big American Telescopes*. Tucson: University of Arizona Press, 1993.

Page, Susanne, and Jake Page. *Hopi*. New York: Henry N. Abrams, 1982.

———. *Navajo*. Tucson: Rio Nuevo, 2010.

Pattie, James Ohio. *The Personal Narrative of James Ohio Pattie of Kentucky*. Edited by Timothy Flint and Reuben Gold Thwaites. Cleveland, OH: Arthur C. Clark, 1905.

Poling-Kempes, Lesley. *The Harvey Girls: Women Who Opened the West*. New York: Paragon House, 1994.

Porter, Eliot. *The Place No One Knew*. San Francisco: Sierra Club Books, 1963.

Powell, James Lawrence. *Grand Canyon: Solving Earth's Grandest Puzzle*. New York: Penguin, 2005.

Powell, John Wesley. *The Arid Lands*. Edited by Wallace Stegner. Lincoln: University of Nebraska Press, 2004.

———. *The Exploration of the Colorado River and Its Canyons*. New York: Viking Penguin, 1987.

Priestley, J. B. *Midnight on the Desert: Being an Excursion into Autobiography During a Winter in America, 1935–36.* New York: Harper and Brothers, 1937.

Pyne, Stephen J. *How the Canyon Became Grand: A Short History.* New York: Penguin, 1998.

Quartaroli, Richard D., ed. *A Rendezvous of Grand Canyon Historians: Ideas, Arguments, and First-Person Accounts; Proceedings of the Third Grand Canyon History Symposium, January 2012.* Grand Canyon: Grand Canyon Association, 2013.

Ranney, Wayne. *Carving Grand Canyon: Evidence, Theories, and Mystery.* 2nd ed. Grand Canyon: Grand Canyon Association, 2012.

Reilly, P. T. *Lee's Ferry: From Mormon Crossing to National Park.* Logan: Utah State University Press, 1999.

Renehan, Edward. *John Burroughs: An American Naturalist.* Hensonville, NY: Black Dome Press, 1998.

Richmond, Al. *Cowboys, Miners, Presidents, and Kings: The Story of the Grand Canyon Railway.* Williams, AZ: Grand Canyon Railway, 1989.

Roosevelt, Theodore. *A Book Lover's Holiday in the Open.* New York: Charles Scribner's Sons, 1919.

Runte, Alfred. *National Parks: The American Experience.* Lanham, MD: Taylor Trade, 2010.

Russell, Herbert K. *Edgar Lee Masters: A Biography.* Urbana: University of Illinois Press, 2001.

Sandburg, Carl. *The Complete Poems of Carl Sandburg.* New York: Harcourt Brace Jovanovich, 1970.

Santa Fe Railway. *The Grand Canyon of Arizona.* Chicago: Santa Fe Railway, 1902.

Schullery, Paul, ed. *The Grand Canyon: Early Impressions.* Boulder, CO: Pruett, 1989.

Shanklin, Robert. *Steve Mather of the National Parks.* New York: Alfred A. Knopf, 1951.

Shepherd, Jeffrey P. *We Are an Indian Nation: A History of the Hualapai People.* Tucson: University of Arizona Press, 2010.

Spamer, Earle. "Once Again, 'Who Named the Grand Canyon?'—and Other Grand Canyon 'Firsts.'" *Ol' Pioneer* (Spring 2013).

Stanton, Robert Brewster. *The Colorado River Survey: Robert B. Stanton and the Denver, Colorado Canyon, and Pacific Railroad.* Edited by Dwight L. Smith and C. Gregory Crampton. Salt Lake City: Howe Brothers, 1987.

———. *Down the Colorado.* Edited by Dwight L. Smith. Norman: University of Oklahoma Press, 1965.

Stegner, Wallace. *Beyond the Hundredth Meridian: John Wesley Powell and the Second Opening of the West.* Boston: Houghton Mifflin, 1953.

Steinbeck, John. *"America and Americans," and Selected Nonfiction.* Edited by Susan Shillinglaw and Jackson J. Benson. New York: Viking, 2002.

Sterling, George. *Sonnets to Craig.* Long Beach, CA: Albert and George Boni, 1928.

Stone, Julius. *Canyon Country: The Romance of a Drop of Water and a Grain of Sand.* New York: G. P. Putnam's Sons, 1932.

Supplee, Serena. *Inner Gorge Metaphors: An Artist's Perspective of the Grand Canyon.* Moab, UT: Lily Canyon Books, 2005.

Suran, William C. *The Kolb Brothers of Grand Canyon.* Grand Canyon: Grand Canyon Natural History Association, 1991.

Swain, Donald C. *Wilderness Defender: Horace M. Albright and Conservation.* Chicago: University of Chicago Press, 1970.

Teague, David W. *The Southwest in American Literature and Art: The Rise of a Desert Aesthetic.* Tucson: University of Arizona Press, 1997.

Teal, Louise. *Breaking into the Current: Boatwomen of the Grand Canyon.* Tucson: University of Arizona Press, 1994.

Tillotson, Miner, and Frank J. Taylor. *Grand Canyon Country.* Stanford, CA: Stanford University Press, 1929.

Van Dyke, Henry. *The Grand Canyon, and Other Poems.* New York: Charles Scribner's Sons, 1914.

Van Dyke, John C. *The Desert: Further Studies in Natural Appearances.* Baltimore: Johns Hopkins University Press, 1999.

———. *The Grand Canyon of the Colorado.* New York: Charles Scribner's Sons, 1927.

Verkamp, Margaret M. *History of Grand Canyon National Park.* Flagstaff, AZ: Grand Canyon Pioneers Society, 1993.

Walker, Dale L. *Rough Rider: Buckey O'Neill of Arizona.* Lincoln: University of Nebraska Press, 1997.

Warner, Charles Dudley. *Our Italy.* New York: Harper and Brothers, 1891.

Watkins, T. H. *Righteous Pilgrim: The Life and Times of Harold L. Ickes, 1874–1952.* New York: Henry Holt, 1990.

Webb, Roy. *Call of the Colorado.* Moscow: University of Idaho Press, 1994.

Welch, Vince. *The Last Voyageur: Amos Burg and the Rivers of the West.* Seattle: Mountaineers Books, 2012.

Welch, Vince, Cort Conley, and Brad Dimock. *The Doing of the Thing: The Brief Whitewater Career of Buzz Holmstrom.* Flagstaff, AZ: Fretwater Press, 1998.

Westwood, Richard. *Woman of the River: Georgie White Clark, Whitewater Pioneer.* Logan: Utah State University Press, 1997.

Wilhelms, Don E. *To a Rocky Moon: A Geologist's History of Lunar Exploration.* Tucson: University of Arizona Press, 1993.

Wilkins, Thurman. *Artist of the Mountains.* Norman: University of Oklahoma Press, 1966.

Williams, Ellen. *Harriet Monroe and the Poetry Renaissance: The First Ten Years of Poetry, 1912–1922.* Urbana: University of Illinois Press, 1977.

Winship, George Parker, trans. and ed. *The Journey of Coronado, 1540–1542.* Golden, CO: Fulcrum, 1990.

Worster, Donald. *A Passion for Nature: The Life of John Muir.* New York: Oxford University Press, 2008.

———. *A River Running West: The Life of John Wesley Powell.* New York: Oxford University Press, 2001.

Yochelson, Ellis L. *Charles Doolittle Walcott, Paleontologist.* Kent, OH: Kent State University Press, 1998.

Index